DRAGON'S MOUTH

DRAGON'S MOUTH

A Dramatic Quartet in Two Parts

by JACQUETTA HAWKES
and
J. B. PRIESTLEY

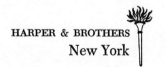

HARPER & BROTHERS
New York

DRAGON'S MOUTH

FIRST EDITION

L - E

Library of Congress catalog card number: 55-12371

CONTENTS

PROLOGUE

I SPENT the late autumn of 1951 in New York, where I had gone to do a play. My old friend, Sir Cedric Hardwicke, arrived in the city, for the Charles Laughton production of Shaw's *Don Juan in Hell*, in which Sir Cedric had been playing for many months, had now found its way to the Atlantic. He asked me to dine at the Algonquin and suggested that after dinner I should cross with him to Brooklyn, where he was performing in the Shaw piece that night. I hesitated. I felt no desire to renew acquaintance with this particular chunk of Shaw, and I imagined that Charles Laughton's production of it (which had been rather sourly noticed in England during the summer) was a stunt affair, designed to exploit film stars. But finally I agreed to go to Brooklyn; and out of this decision *Dragon's Mouth* may be said to have been born.

The Brooklyn auditorium was crowded, mostly with eager youngish folk, of a type one does not see often in New York. It was the kind of audience I like. The production was extremely adroit and the acting uncommonly good. I knew what Charles Laughton and Sir Cedric could do, so there was no surprise here, but I was astounded by the range and force of Charles Boyer's performance as Juan. The hold of the piece and the players on the audience was wonderful. The

vii

laughter and applause came far more easily than they do in the ordinary theater. One of Shaw's most difficult scenes, containing some of the longest speeches he ever wrote, was playing here like a house on fire. These performers in evening clothes, pretending to read and using no scenery, costume, make-up, stage lighting, created a feeling of freshness, zest, attack, to which the audience immediately responded. It made recent stage plays I had seen appear by comparison so many faded masquerades. I found myself losing interest in the play I had gone to New York to do. Here was something new and exciting, a production almost reduced to a bare platform, that brought both the dramatist and the actors much closer to the audience, I felt, than they were in the ordinary theater. This was no stunt. There might be here the beginning of a new and powerful form of writing, producing, acting.

While all those young and enthusiastic Brooklyn folk were still applauding, I hurried out to go backstage and tell Charles Laughton what I had been feeling about his experiment. He gave me one of his huge knowing grins, in which the extremes of innocence and sophistication seem blended. He told me they had to go away again for two or three weeks but after that would be opening for a short season at the Century Theatre, New York, which fortunately was just round the corner from my hotel. I replied that he would find me there.

So there I was, when the Drama Quartet came to the Century Theatre; and I had several discussions with Charles, who explained what he thought might be done with this form of production while I suggested possible themes that might be adapted for treatment

in such a manner. From these discussions I learned
much that was of great service to me when I came to
produce *Dragon's Mouth* myself later. I discovered too
it had been thought all along that if I found this
method attractive I was a writer who might contribute
something that could be successfully produced more
or less in the same style. So I agreed to have a try,
and possible ideas for platform drama began to buzz
around in my mind. Incidentally, by this time I had
lost all interest in the ordinary theater job I had originally gone out there to do.

I had also found a most valuable and distinguished
collaborator. It was after one of the performances at
the Century Theatre that I ran into Jacquetta
Hawkes, then returning from visits to Harvard and
Yale. She had felt much the same as I had done about
this production of *Don Juan in Hell,* and when I told
her that I believed there was somewhere here the basis
of a new form of dramatic writing, she was in enthusiastic agreement. So I invited her to collaborate with
me. As an old hand in the theater, I could supply the
purely dramatic ideas, the framework and construction, while she could lend to our joint enterprise those
gifts, so original, intelligent, deeply poetic, that had
shone in *A Land.* I will confess now that I was doubtful whether her strong clean prose, so admirable to
read to oneself, could be successfully spoken and de-
claimed on platform or stage; but I took the chance,
risking the possibility of embittered arguments on the
difference between literary and dramatic style. There
were no such arguments, and indeed most of the
speeches that have aroused the enthusiasm of *Dragon's
Mouth* audiences were hers and not mine. And I will

add here that whatever the merits or faults of this piece might be, it does remain, I think, an unusually successful example of collaboration between two writers with very different temperaments, backgrounds, manners and styles.

There was time, before I left New York, to sketch the dramatic framework of the piece and to agree about the four characters in it. The solid work had to be done between us back in London, after Christmas. We divided the four characters equally between us, at least for their long speeches (most of the linking dialogue was originally mine, though each of us revised if necessary the work of the other); and this plan enabled us to work hard and fast. (Please note that we did not divide these characters according to our own sex but each took a man and a woman. Some critics have been caught out by this unexpected division, blaming or praising each of us for the other's work.) Here it is necessary to say that what spurred us on was the belief that here was an interesting new form. Yet because we acknowledged the debt to Laughton's production of a Shaw piece, there has been a confusion that has had irritating results in some notices of *Dragon's Mouth,* notices in which Shaw was dragged in for comparison, usually of course most unfavorable to ourselves. (The very type of dramatic critics who kept Shaw out of the theater for years now use him as a stick with which to assault later dramatists.) Shaw simply does not come into this picture. We did not aspire to write like Shaw. I had some modest acquaintance with him, and I am certain he would have detested *Dragon's Mouth* even as an experiment, for while he believed in and created the drama of debate, he had a marked taste for old-fashioned theatrical effects—characters in gorgeous uniforms or fancy dress, operetta scenic displays, interludes of knockabout comic business. No, it was not the Shavian content but the Laughton method in *Don Juan in Hell* that first fascinated us and then inspired us to experiment with this form.

There were differences, of course. We dropped all pretense of reading, the feature of the Laughton production I had liked least. After the impersonal exposition at the beginning of our piece, there were no further descriptions of what was happening; the characters behaved as they might have done in an ordinary stage play. Our actors wore evening clothes, but then the characters they were playing might also have been wearing such clothes. We designed an unpretentious arrangement of microphone stands and white ropes that suggested our scene, the deck of a yacht. We used a few offstage effects—the hooting of a distant steamer, a gong, the noise of an approaching motorboat. We made a few modest changes of lighting during the performance, and ended with quite a marked dramatic change. We had all this in view during our writing of the script. When I came to produce the piece I designed the production so that it could easily be performed in halls of various shapes and sizes, although we opened our tour in a theater, the Malvern Festival Theatre, and concluded it by occupying the Winter Garden Theatre in Drury Lane, where I made an effective use of the apron stage that had been built over the orchestra pit. For my part, however, I preferred to see the production in a hall of reasonable shape and dimensions. It seemed to me more exciting to see and hear this platform piece away from a proscenium and curtains, with its own lighting, screens, little arrangement of mikes and ropes, converting a town hall into a new kind of theater.

Here I must defend our use of mikes and amplified sound. It is not true, as many people seem to have imagined, that we needed them simply because we were often playing in very large halls with bad acoustics. Certainly they were necessary in such halls, and indeed almost everywhere on our one-night stands. But these people were wrong in thinking that we could do without the amplified sound as soon as we arrived in a theater. Our actors of course were quite capable of making themselves heard in any theater. But that is not the point. Our method of production depended upon the use of mikes and amplified sound. Our performers had to be able to talk intimately, without the "projection" necessary in the theater, and then make long speeches that ranged from whispers to thundering oratory, all without the least strain on the hearing of the audience. Many of these people who condemned our use of amplified sound were yet astonished that we were able to keep our audiences so quietly attentive for such lengthy periods; they failed to understand the connection between this method of production and the behavior of audiences. But it was there, and without the mikes we could never have dominated the audience in this fashion. Moreover, I tried to make use of the mikes themselves for obtaining certain dramatic effects, giving queer tones to the voice. Finally, the anchoring of each character to his or her mike, only making a move away from them to heighten the scene, was an essential part of the production.

I am an impatient man, always have been and now, it seems, always will be. I cannot bear waiting long for anything good to happen. I have never been able, as superior beings are able, to plan far ahead, to settle today what I shall be doing in two or three years' time. I rush at everything—even work. So no sooner had we received enthusiastic cables from Charles Laughton and his business partner, Paul Gregory, about the script of *Dragon's Mouth* we had sent them, than I must produce it here in England. It had to be done at once, could not wait until the autumn, because I expected to be in America and the Far East by that time. The truth is, I was longing to produce it, to discover for myself how audiences would receive it, to make the experiment not merely on paper but in actual halls; and in my haste I overlooked one important fact. I knew that this new form demanded a new way of writing, of producing, of acting, but what I overlooked was the fact that a production of this kind would have to be *sold* to the public in an equally brand-new fashion. And the further fact that however this was to be done, it could not be done properly in a few weeks but needed careful organization and probably several months' preparation. What I needed badly was an impresario, an eager but efficient showman, who would leave me free to concentrate upon the casting and production while he booked the halls, found some adequate method of selling tickets, arranged transport, and worked up the publicity. Now that our experiment has attracted so much attention, I gather there are several enthusiasts who would have been delighted to act as our showman, but while everything was still on paper no such impresario suggested himself. With the result that while I was busy rehearsing—and rehearsing this type of production, though delightful, is extremely hard work—I had to improvise some sort of organization, usually toiling at it early in the morning and late at night; and with the further and more horrible consequence that, booking our halls at such short notice and in such a blank state of ignorance about them and their ticket agents, we finally set out to entertain people who often had never heard of us and to do it often in halls that nobody in his senses would have booked for this or any other kind of entertainment.

We made no attempt to cover the country, and indeed never went near some of our largest cities and most promising audiences. But I ought to have remembered—for I had had some experience of concert touring with the London Philharmonic—that England, unlike America (where Laughton had made his triumphant progress), is desperately short of good halls, especially large halls in the industrial towns. It would, in my view, be comparatively easy to organize a successful tour of "a platform piece" in smaller towns, on a sort of Number Two Company touring basis, but a Number One Company, with star performers and a heavy salary list, may find it hard to book an adequate number of good large halls. Except where our publicity and ticket-selling arrangements were hopelessly ineffectual, we found that the size of our audience was proportionate to the esteem in which the local hall was held. Thus, in Bristol, where they are proud of their Colston Hall, we had a magnificent audience, whereas in Coventry, where nobody seemed to know where our hall was, we played to a pitiful sprinkling of people. In addition, some new method of selling tickets, possibly based on local playgoers' and other cultural organizations, must be devised, and ample time must be allowed both for publicity and the sale of tickets. My gallant publishers and I learnt a great deal about touring this kind of production on one-night stands, but we learnt it the hard way.

Fortunately our four players, who had had a tough time both memorizing their lines and reversing much of their stage technique, and our stage staff, who lived desperate lives on tour, were with us body, heart and soul. I will repeat here what I have declared before— that in this experiment it was from the theater people themselves that I received the most eager and enthusiastic co-operation. I have done my share of grumbling at actors, but I have never yet made any experiment in the theater when they were not my best allies. If our theater tends too often to be unprogressive, stale, routine in ideas and technique, it is not the fault of our performers, who are only too anxious to try something new and exciting, even at the risk of failure (serious for them) and ridicule. It is not the actors who get into a groove and want to stay there. If managers, theater owners, press and public, were only half so willing to welcome something new, we should have far more challenging and memorable evenings in the playhouse than we have at present. We met enthusiasts everywhere—and I shall have something to say about our audiences later—but more than once I was rather shocked to discover how the very people who grumble because everything seems so stale and routine these days, who demand something new and original, were also the people who did nothing whatever to help our enterprise and cast doubts upon it before they made its acquaintance. Too many of us English, I suspect, have arrived at the hopeless position of being weary of what is old and well-tried while still being suspicious and grudging about anything that is new and adventurous, thus making the worst of both worlds.

Our audiences may not always have been as large as we had hoped—and everybody told us our publicity was bad—but there could be no doubt about their response. The dramatic experiment succeeded: we fired a shot into the dark—and *ping!*—there was the target. People listened with an intentness rarely felt now in the theater. The storms of coughing that generally accompany any long and thoughtful speech had been banished. Without most of the usual theatrical devices and aids, the piece seized and held their imagination. And these were audiences, as I saw for myself, from many different backgrounds—industrial, resort, university—yet in only one respect did their responses vary. Some audiences insisted upon applauding at the end of the more impressive long speeches, whereas other audiences kept quiet until the end of the act. (And as people have asked me about this, I might as well reply here that I prefer occasional "rounds" to a continued silence. They relieve the tension for both performers and audience. Listening is easier, as concert goers know, if you are allowed now and again to make a noise yourself.) We had hoped that audiences, finding themselves often directly addressed, would feel closer to the characters and their dramatic situation and their various revelations than they did in the familiar playhouse. We had hoped that they would find themselves caught up in our arguments, moved to agreement or sharp protest by our more oratorical passages. We had hoped that the personalities of the actors (and this form demands good acting) would be seen in a clearer light. And what we had hoped came true. Of course both in London and the provinces a few critics told us that this was not a play (forgetting that we had said it first) and one or two, possibly intellectual giants condemned mysteriously to write short theatrical notices in popular papers, complained that we were platitudinous and boring. But on the whole the response from both press and public was far more enthusiastic than I had ever imagined it would be.

It is all too easy to be portentous about a little experiment of this sort. I will try to retain a sense of proportion. Our object was not to challenge the ordinary theater, which can do many things superbly well that these platform pieces could not even attempt. But there seems to me a place for this kind of dramatic writing and production. Radio has given people a taste for debate, the clash of opinion and ideas. But radio has also robbed people of oratory, if only because in politics the broadcast talk in the fireside manner has driven out impassioned platform speeches in the grand manner. And here is a new form that combines debate and oratory, while setting them both, as I believe it should, in a dramatic framework. Much of the old magic of the playhouse is lost, but in place of that there is a decided gain in the more direct appeal of this form, in the closer participation of the audience in the production. I would agree that this is not entirely new, for there is something like a return here to Clas-

sical and Elizabethan Drama. What is new is the use
of cunningly amplified sound, which recent develop-
ments have made possible. With a good sound system
and a portable switchboard and lights, any hall can
be transformed into a playhouse of sorts for this form
of writing and production; and the essential magic of
the theater is not lost but is given an opportunity to
weave its spells in a new fashion, closer perhaps to
some of the needs of our time, with its concern for
opinion and ideas, its hunger for a style that is at least
superior to the drab patter of the newspapers and the
radio program. Here is a method of presentation so
flexible that it can be enjoyed by four thousand people
in a great concert hall or by fifty people in a village
institute. Yet personality has not been sacrificed, for
if such pieces are well contrived and written and
properly produced and acted, the personalities of
writers, producers, performers, are even more sharply
revealed than usual. So here then is something to set
against the vast standardization and monopoly of television. I believe that these platform pieces are not easy
to devise and write, are hard to produce and act well,
and that they demand a great deal of efficient organization (to which I lay no claim), together with much
enthusiasm on the part of everybody concerned with
them. Perhaps we are all feeling too tired and stale to
bother about them. But I am glad some of us had a try.

J. B. PRIESTLEY

DRAGON'S MOUTH

CHARACTERS

MATTHEW

STUART

NINA

HARRIET

PART ONE

*(The four performers come on together, either with
house lights still on or with house lights down but
all spots on. After bowing to the applause they seat
themselves before their respective microphones.
Then, a recorded voice, with a deep weighty impersonal tone, comes through the speakers.)*

RECORDED VOICE

Ladies and Gentlemen—*Dragon's Mouth.* There
were four of them; they were on a yacht, *Lucinda*—
about two hundred and fifty tons, carrying four offi-
cers, a wireless operator, and a crew of eight. The
owner of the yacht was Matthew—

(here MATTHEW *rises, but not as if listening to the
voice but as if unaware of it)*

a rich man, two of whose companies operate in Venezuela and the West Indies, so that he often ran down
there in his yacht, working and making holiday together. With him was his wife—Nina—

(she now rises and can pretend to talk to MATTHEW,
who can reply in dumb show)

whose photograph you may have often seen, for she
was quite a figure in the world of wealth and fashion.

3

Then there was Stuart, an old friend of Nina's and a scholar and man of letters—

(STUART *rises and joins in the dumb show*)

and, to complete the quartet, Harriet, also a friend but employed by one of Matthew's companies as personnel manager.

(HARRIET *now rises and the four are in position. The dumb show should not be fussy but should suggest that the scene is now alive.*)

Matthew had had some business to do in Maracaibo, Venezuela, and then the yacht was headed for Port of Spain, Trinidad. But one of the crew died, and two of the others were very sick men. A radio message was sent to the medical authorities at Port of Spain, and then the yacht received instructions to find a sheltered anchorage in the passage between Venezuela and Trinidad, the one called Dragon's Mouth. A port doctor came out in a motor launch and took blood samples. He told these four to keep away from the others—on the main deck for'ard. He would let them know the result of his tests as soon as possible, sending a radio message by short wave. So there they were, the four of them, Matthew, Nina, Harriet, Stuart, standing by the rail on the main deck for'ard, waiting for news. . . .

(*The scene now comes alive, with all four staring out as people do at sea. Note: in this quartet,* NINA *is the soprano,* HARRIET *the contralto,* STUART *the tenor,* MATTHEW *the bass. Both* NINA *and* STUART *speak with a delicate precision, a not unpleasant affectation.* HARRIET *and* MATTHEW *are plainer but speak with more warmth and enthusiasm. For all the longer speeches a heightened style of de-*

4

livery is used, and they are spoken more to the audience than to the other characters. Sometimes they sit—at times chosen by the producer—but at the opening they must be all standing, looking out into the evening.)

STUART

Now at last we're free to notice that the evening—unlike our immediate prospects—is perfect. What irony there is in this stillness, the soft dying fall of the sky, the tropical perfumes blowing across the sea! I'm not sure, though, that at this moment I have enough sense of humor to appreciate such irony.

NINA

I've never enjoyed irony—it's as much an acquired taste as caviar—and I'm certainly not amused by it now. But is it such a perfect evening? I seem to detect some touches of malice. All that pale phosphorescence down in the water—it might be the hair of swimming ghosts! And even the moon seems to have turned against us, to be staring at us with a cold Inquisitor's eye. Don't you think so, Harriet darling?

HARRIET

It's the selfsame moon you were worshiping last night. But if you want something threatening, look there—where the sun went down.

STUART

Those rocks silhouetted against the red sky? They look like a jaw full of ragged teeth with one sharp fang among them. . . .

MATTHEW

Well, after all, they call this Dragon's Mouth.

NINA

It's the mouth of hell. And we are the souls awaiting judgment.

HARRIET

Bodies rather. Matthew, didn't the doctor say *any-thing*?

MATTHEW

No, except that we'd have to wait. I don't suppose there was anything he *could* say.

NINA

Why not? At least he might have guessed something.

STUART

My dear Nina, men of science aren't allowed to guess. A doctor is a man who has to send for a colleague to be told he's got a headache. But give him a microscope and he's all confidence and certainty.

NINA

They can't allow themselves the luxury of intuition, although I must say that this man seemed to have an intuition that we weren't very nice people. There was no waiting for scientific evidence of that. He looked at us with a hostile eye as soon as he stepped on board.

MATTHEW

My dear, he's worried, and you can't blame him. God

6

knows what we may have picked up and brought with us. Yellow fever. Bubonic plague. Anything.

NINA

Matthew darling, I wish you wouldn't be so horribly explicit.

HARRIET

Why not? We might as well face the facts. Three of the crew have been attacked by some contagious disease. And there's no particular reason why we four should be immune. Our money, clothes and superior social habits are no protection.

STUART

Certainly they are. Our chances are much better than the crew's. We're cleaner and better nourished, and so more likely to resist infection. Moreover, unlike them, we haven't been boozing and whoring in the stews of Maracaibo. So the odds are in our favor, and I refuse to be worried.

NINA

That's the first comfortable thing you've said today, Stuart.

MATTHEW

I'm not worried really, except about this quarantine business. I hate having my plans wrecked like this.

NINA

You also hate having a blood test. Both you men were very near fainting when the doctor laid hands on you.

7

STUART

I don't like blood—not even my own. I prefer to forget it's there.

HARRIET

If you were a woman—

STUART (*cutting in*)

Yes, I know, I know. But then I'm not a woman—and no other single fact about my existence has given me more continued satisfaction.

MATTHEW

That's a pitiful sort of observation. What a career for a man—just thanking God he's not a woman!

STUART

I didn't say it was my career. I haven't a career. I'm the only truly detached non-careerist here.

NINA

What about me?

STUART

My dear Nina! All those gossip paragraphs, those interviews, those photographs in the glossier magazines! Nina, the smiling guest! Nina, the radiant hostess! Merely having to make it appear, as you do, that you're enjoying a Hunt Ball or a night club, is a career—

HARRIET

A man has just died in this yacht. And two others may die.

8

STUART

I don't think it's necessary to remind us of those grim facts, Harriet. And I doubt if we can improve the next hour or two by brooding over them.

HARRIET

No, but we can be serious for a minute. Matthew, I suppose the doctor took those two men away, didn't he?

MATTHEW

Yes. Rushed them to an isolation hospital. As you know, he didn't say much. But I gather he didn't think they'd much of a chance.

HARRIET

That poor young red-haired man who died—Burgess, wasn't it?—he hadn't a chance at all. The speed of the thing was frightful.

NINA

I can't keep him out of my mind. When I came out on deck yesterday morning, he was up at the masthead. He'd swarmed up just for the devil of the thing to free the pennon. Then he was—with his coppery hair—spread-eagled against the sky. I watched him and thought how splendid he looked. Then before sunset he was on the deck in convulsions—

STUART

Yes, no longer human but a piece of biological machinery making beastly noises as it breaks down.

9

MATTHEW

He was still making a fight of it—poor Burgess!

HARRIET (*after pause*)

You can see how in these horribly hot countries a people would get the idea of a jealous God. Even fatal diseases are more temperate with us. But here we have seen how "The Lord smote him down."

STUART

And it's much easier to accept if you *can* see it that way. The Lord smites poor little Burgess because Burgess has offended Him. Well, at least that boosts the human sense of self-importance. We're *somebody*, if only to be smitten down. But look where we've arrived nowadays, with all our recent cleverness. What an idea of our helpless disintegration it's left us to face! Let us consider you, my dear Nina. Do you mind?

NINA

Go on. It won't make me feel much worse and may make you feel better.

STUART

Certainly. Now here you are, my dear Nina, so delicious in this light, a lovely lady contained in your smooth white skin and shining silks. Nina—who is known in half the fashionable drawing rooms of Western Europe and America, whose features are readily identified in the more expensive magazines of both these continents. No other woman, we feel, has just that exquisite relation between the untroubled brow,

10

the delicious nose, the narrow subtle mouth. As they recognize these unique features, people cry, "There's Nina." I too have studied the geography of your face, my dear, and know its every cape and bay. I too have cried, with delighted recognition, "Here's Nina." But suppose we look closer, look with greater penetration, using the thick spectacles of the scientifically trained intellect. What do we find then, my friends? Why, that this dear and familiar Nina has vanished. She has turned into a vast humming city, into an ant heap. She is no more than a million million cells all living independently, all capable of surviving her. Some are grouped into the busy community of the liver, some are toiling away in the heart, and others are hurrying down the long boulevards of the intestines. All have their communal interests and know nothing of this Nina person. Moreover, let me remind you that at this very moment there may be some foreign agents who have stolen into that cell city, meeting in secret groups, slipping along its red streets. Like the rest of us, they are ruthless, intent only on their own survival. Even now they may be stealing along these thoroughfares planning a final *coup d'état*, a plot to take over the city for their own purposes. Meanwhile, Nina, if she ever existed, has now disintegrated. The habitués of the drawing rooms, the readers of the magazines, will know her no more.

MATTHEW

All of which, even if true, would have been better left unsaid.

NINA

It doesn't worry me, darling.

HARRIET

And *I* don't think it's true. It's mere cleverness con-
juring up its own idea of death. Oh—I don't pretend I
can still picture the soul as an imaginable thing, carried up to Heaven by angels holding the four corners
of a cloth. But I still believe that everyone has some
individual presence, some king who rules over this
city of cells. There's something in us, belonging to another order of being, that can't be identified with all
this material stuff and its processes.

MATTHEW

Of course. And at heart we all know it. Besides, all
this bogy-bogy talk of cities of cells and foreign agents
is a mere trick of metaphor. I've noticed it before in
popular articles by scientists, who can't stop trying to
make our flesh creep and have been at it ever since
they first went home and told their baby sisters they'd
been dissecting frogs. Stuart can't have it both ways.
If the cells of our bodies are to be promoted into citi-
zens and foreign agents, given a human status, then
we don't disappear but must be promoted too—raised
into gods. On the other hand, if we're still human, then
our body cells are so far below the human scale that
it's completely false to describe them as he did, as if
they had a human will and purpose. I don't propose to
be cheated out of my individuality by any such half-
baked thinking.

NINA

You and Harriet are both so accustomed to using
your own authority and to the strength and weight of
your personalities that you could hardly think anything else. I don't believe it has ever happened to

12

either of you in all your lives to feel helpless, to know you're in the grip of the universe. Try having a baby, then you'd know that you're just an agent of Nature. Lie in your bath and observe how each week your belly rises an inch higher above the water, and also observe, and accept, the fact that you can do nothing to stop it.

HARRIET

That's neither here nor there—you know perfectly well, Nina, you haven't got an argument. But I must confess that my own conviction isn't perfectly rational either. It is a grim experience of my own that makes me certain I'm right. When my father was very old, a year or two before he died, he had a small hemorrhage of the brain, and while it was acute his worn and fouled body lay helpless and silly—he wasn't a human being at all. But when the clot had been absorbed, then his personality returned. He told us that he'd known all that happened while he had seemed to be away. He gave us the names of people whom he'd failed to recognize and said that he'd been horribly aware of his own vacancy and had suffered from it. So you see my father had been there all the time, haunting his own body but unable to call out.

NINA

Yes, I see, darling. But don't imagine you're being very comforting.

STUART

Comforting! It's hell. Far worse than anything I've suggested. Better to have no inner self than to be the helpless prisoner of your rebellious body, unable even to give a signal—

MATTHEW

No, it isn't better. You have to run that risk. It's the price you pay for being a person, and not a piece of machinery. The trouble with you, Stuart, is that you never want to pay the price or to run any risk. That's why you don't really live. If any theory or scheme of life makes any sharp demands on you, then you prefer to believe it to be false. You won't take the gamble, so you never accomplish anything. You're lost in despair because everything isn't perfect and given away for nothing. You're like a man who won't dine at all unless the dinner is free and reaches perfection.

STUART

Nothing could be further from the truth. I accept gratefully whatever can be relished and properly digested. It's you, my friend, who've never enjoyed a meal yet, simply because you've always been in such a hurry, so childishly eager, to find the perfect dinner that is always just round the corner. And you bustle the rest of us with you round corner after corner, where we find less and less to enjoy. Certainly you've accomplished something. You've helped to bring into existence the modern world, and it's doubtful if men have ever had a worse one.

NINA

My poor Matthew!

STUART

Whereas I, for my part, have always fully enjoyed what is possible for a man of taste to enjoy, while

14

keeping his intelligence free and critical, giving no blank checks to self-deception.

HARRIET

And I don't believe there's any real happiness in it.

STUART

Oh—come, come, Harriet. You can't deny that I know how to savor life—

HARRIET

As soon as people talk about savoring life, I know they're mere self-indulgent tasters. Life has to be lived and not savored. It's not a roast partridge or a glass of claret. Life—

NINA

No, darling, I loathe those large vague statements about life. Besides you've cut short Stuart when he's still longing to tell us about his pleasures. I for one shall be very glad to listen. Here we are, waiting in the night to hear whether we're normal people or creatures to be hurried away into isolation and distress, like prisoners waiting while the jury finds a verdict. So let Stuart stage his exquisite show—even if it's only for comfort's sake.

STUART

Thank you, Nina. I feel as you do. Well now—are you listening, Harriet?

HARRIET

Yes, and waiting to be converted.

15

STUART

My dear, that's your trouble—you've always been waiting to be converted. I neither want to be converted nor to convert. This complete absence of conversion is part of my charm. But now—leave this scented darkness, this glittering but melancholy ocean, and let me show you how I live—how I have chosen to live. Here I am, in my rooms, sitting in my study, and knowing perfect satisfaction. My evening meal was frugal perhaps, but well-chosen, admirably cooked and served. I am now turning it into scholarship, possibly into literature, but am not aware of the process. My idle glances stray over the shelves, rippling along the colored corrugated backs of my books; I am half aware of their precious contents, of their authors. I look again at my favorite possessions, at that lovely fragment of a smiling head, an archaic piece that I brought back from Naxos; and I think of my own past journeys and of the golden times when such things were made. I hear the noise of the traffic outside my chambers, and the walls seem to draw nearer, to enclose me, not in the prison of our age but in whatever period of the life of man that pleases me. The light from my lamp pours onto the desk where I have been writing. My Siamese cat, like some half-savage queen now my guest, stretches and delicately yawns. My bracket clock strikes midnight. Shall I go to bed or compose another sentence or two? It does not matter. I can please myself. I am perfectly contented.

NINA

Dear Stuart, how charming! I can almost smell the

16

smoke of your beautiful cigars and see the sour-apple-green pattern of your Chinese rug.

STUART

Thank you, my dear Nina.

MATTHEW

But, Nina, you told me you'd never been inside Stuart's rooms.

NINA

Darling, I was lying. I'm devoted to you, as you must know, but sometimes I tell you lies. You're not the kind of man a woman can be truthful with all the time.

STUART

Are there such men?

NINA

Yes, a great many—but not among my friends, because they are too dull. They are the safe men—as safe as houses and far less interesting. They can't earn the compliment of a lie.

MATTHEW

Well, I suppose I must be reassured if you think me dangerous.

STUART

Yes, you are a fortunate man, she is still just decently afraid of you. But let us return to myself. Now I have given you some idea of how I like to live—only a slight indication, of course—what do you think of it?

17

MATTHEW

It's an admirable existence for a man of eighty-five
—or even for a man of seventy if he should be recover-
ing from the flu. But as a real man's life, I don't think
much of it.

NINA

I think I'd be more impressed, Stuart, if I didn't
know you. Forgive me—but—somehow the result
isn't very exciting.

STUART

But then I've never had the least desire to be exciting. Being very much of a woman, my dear Nina, you
are at heart an animal trainer—eagerly exploring the
jungle of men to bring some back alive—and I'm too
far removed from the male gorilla to challenge your
skill. But, Harriet, I appeal to you. Admit that I'm
discriminating but not narrow, and that I do enjoy
the feast of life.

HARRIET

No, not the feast. Only the hors d'oeuvres, prepared
by a clever chef from scores of little dishes pillaged
from every country and every age. You relish them
one after another, picking them up on the point of
your sharp mind, forever selecting, tasting, judging.
But never feasting. You are always alone with your
palate.

STUART

Certainly I am. What do you propose we should have
—a communal palate, one to every block of tenements?

HARRIET

No, but what I do propose is that we shouldn't talk about enjoying the feast of life when what we really mean is cautious selfish tasting. A real feast ought to be a kind of communion. We have to share it with other people.

STUART

And no doubt all of them selfless servants of the common good, hot and perspiring with devotion and love. Well, if that's your feast, certainly you must leave me out. I prefer a little bread and cheese elsewhere.

HARRIET

Exactly. You see, Stuart, you don't enjoy other people, you only enjoy yourself.

STUART

And so does everybody else. The very phrase gives us away. We don't ask, "Did you enjoy your relationship with your loving fellow creatures, last night?" We say, "Did you enjoy yourself last night?"

NINA

Very neat, Stuart, and I agree with you. But I'm not sure you have much of a self to enjoy. It's chiefly your own cleverness you enjoy, and I suspect that becomes very dusty after a time. I believe that of the four of us, I'm the only one who can really be happy. Harriet is too conscientious, emotional, self-sacrificing. Stuart is too intellectual and finicky. Matthew is too ambitious, too busy, always desperately arranging to arrive somewhere quite different, where life will really begin.

And happiness is in the moment, the actual living present, nowhere else, and I know how to find it there. That's what's always attracted you, isn't it, Matthew darling?

MATTHEW

Yes it is, my dear.

STUART

Don't give in to her like that, man.

MATTHEW

I'm not giving in to her. She's quite right. A man like me needs a woman like Nina to complete him—just as you probably need a cat—and one of the chief ways in which she completes him is by finding happiness where he can't find it—in the moment, as she calls it, and in little things that suddenly set her eyes blazing. Why, I've seen a few roses turn Nina into a lighthouse. And to me that's wonderful, that's magic.

STUART

And do you need magic?

MATTHEW

Certainly I do. You don't understand me. Don't imagine because I've made money that I can't be a kind of poet at heart. Remember I've never made money by saving pennies and by cunning little swindles; I've made it by playing my hunches, realizing dreams, bringing something new into the world; and there's poetry in all that, perhaps more than there is in most of the cold-hearted crab-apple belly-aching verses of the poets we have nowadays. Yes,

20

I'm a kind of poet, and what I've always wanted is magic.

HARRIET

That's perfectly true, and it's something I've always known about you.

STUART

Now you're flattering him, my dear Harriet.

HARRIET

I'm not, any more than I'm your dear Harriet. I never flatter people.

STUART

Not even those members of the working class you have to keep in a good temper? No, don't tell me; it wasn't a fair question. But, Matthew, don't mistake yourself. You're no poet, only a giant adolescent still suffering from growing pains. Poets don't really find magic in women. They find it where it belongs—in poetry. Strictly speaking, women have no magic. When you discover any in the neighborhood of one of them, you've brought it with you. Of course, if magic's what you want, they'll pretend to have it, like a shopkeeper uncertain of his wares but desperately anxious for custom.

NINA

I'm relieved to know that at least we're trying to please.

STUART

You flatter men by reflecting what's in their minds.

21

But also you need Man, with his shaping craftsman's brain, to become characters at all.

HARRIET

So we have no characters now—um?

STUART

You have, Harriet my dear, because there are masculine elements in you, chiefly of the emotional sort. But the purely feminine type has no character. So she depends on Man, who hates whatever's shapeless, to give her one. No, what she has is a huge, blundering but ruthless purpose. And it's this combination of characterless mass and adamantine purpose that makes you the most fearsome species on earth. When God plucked out that rib he did his most dangerous action of a very dangerous week.

NINA

I was taught that by my governess. All little girls are taught to feel guilty about Eve. But I knew even then that that wasn't the real story but only something that men had made up among themselves, to account for their supposed superiority and all the fuss about the knowledge of good and evil—

HARRIET

And to establish the masculine idea, with its authority and restrictions and pride and anger, in place of the old matriarchy, which was easy and peaceful and saw all people as children of Earth—

STUART

And kept them for untold ages lurking in the forest; sheltering in caves; mindless and stagnant; without in-

ventions, laws, rational traditions, history and progress; no better than anthropoid apes; merely eating
and sleeping, copulating and gestating; blundering
witlessly from birth to death, generation after generation, until Man, making use of his superior energy
to achieve the conscious mind, awoke out of his long
sleep—and rebelled.

NINA

To find himself shut outside the Garden of Eden.

MATTHEW

But with his work to do, and his knowledge of good
and evil. Sometimes I believe you imagine good and
evil to be the same thing.

NINA

And in the end that may be our greatness, and may
save you yet.

STUART

We have nothing we care for that you could save.

HARRIET

Except your lives.

STUART

I tell you, when I think of Woman I see her alter-
nately as amorphous soggy mass and the huge mindless indestructible purpose: as the swamp, the quaking
bog, capable of swallowing everything original, fine
and delicate; as the mountain peak, icy hard, set apart
in the grim eternity of her purpose, the home of the
cruel White Goddess. With neither have I anything
to do.

NINA

No, not you—you infertile taster of sensations, you picker among the dead bones of life, you monk without a God. I'd never forgive you if I didn't know some woman brought you into the world, in all the pain and tears and blood that you despise.

MATTHEW

She has you there, my fine fellow.

STUART

She has not—and don't sell the pass. Did I ask to come roaring into this world in that dreadful mess of blood and filth. No, a thousand times No!

HARRIET

Out of that blood and filth come all your scholarship, science and art, the last self-portraits of Rembrandt, the later quartets of Beethoven—

STUART

And again I cry *No*. They came from the rebellious spirit of Man that will not be satisfied with this earth. Those self-portraits and later quartets, which I admire and understand better than you do, dear ladies, were created by desperate elderly men long past the comprehension of women, who if they had cared at all would have begged them to do something gay and fashionable, just in time for next season.

MATTHEW

By Jupiter, you're right, my boy. Just when you're ready to bring something new into the world, to justify

24

your existence, the women give you dark bewildered looks and ask you if you've taken your temperature.

STUART

As she artfully reflects his spirit, Woman makes Man believe he sees something rare in her thought, something exciting in her apprehension of the world, but when he goes nearer, his feet sink into the morass, which is waiting to suck down and smother forever all original thought, every fine perception, the whole rebellious masculine spirit. Down into the swamp, back into the Cave!

NINA

Too much theory, too many metaphors. I'm not impressed. You dislike women merely because you would like to make love to them and can't.

STUART

There it goes, there it goes—the jungle retort, the Cave argument. Breed, breed—or perish!

MATTHEW

Still, as Nina's husband, I can't say I'm sorry to hear her charge against you. Though of course, my dear, you could be lying again.

NINA

I could, darling, but I'm not.

STUART

And I tell you, my besotted friend, she hardly knows the difference. Well, Nina, you want some plain truths and here they are. Ever since I first met you in Paris, talking about grouse to a Turkish ambassador (who, incidentally, imagined, as I discovered later, that you were discussing the problem of Trieste), I've wished I could love you, but I've failed. Oh yes—the beauty was there, although even then that beauty is more a product of my mind than of yours.

NINA

I think it's chiefly the joint product of my father and mother, with a few touches added by myself. But where are these plain truths of yours?

STUART

Here. I detest your sex's utter lack of objectivity, your irrelevancies, your evasions. You have no notion of a sense of justice. You are more ruthlessly competitive than the most aggressive males. You have no loyalty among yourselves. You can be jealous and spiteful even when the other woman is enjoying something you've already refused. There's no proportion in your minds. You are insanely angry at a man's trifling physical infidelities but are yourselves sentimentally and spiritually polygamous, almost promiscuous, which is much worse.

MATTHEW

Yes, they're furious if you look at another woman—whom they immediately call *your* Mrs. So-and-so—but they'll keep half a dozen of their own admirers hanging about—

STUART

So many gardeners to water the plant of their vanity. Then you pretend you're doing it from gener-

26

osity and pity, which is never true and merely comes out of your infinite capacity for deluding yourselves. You're ridiculously easily aggrieved—a wrong word, a look, will do it—but then bear the grievance with a horrible nobility. You'll insist upon sacrificing yourselves for some poor devil until he must either take to drink or drop thankfully into the grave. You claim extraordinary credit for bearing children, but half of you will then quietly attempt to eat them alive. More men have been ruined by their mothers than by all the seven deadly sins put together. Until age has made you hideous, you paint and display yourselves to catch every man's eye and inflame him, and then are insulted if you succeed. If we pant after you, we're a nuisance or worse; if we don't, we're probably queer and a scandal. You are idle but ambitious, mean but extravagant, cunning but stupid— Come on, Matthew. Be a man.

MATTHEW

There's no satisfying you, no pleasing you for long. You marry a man because, as you say, he "does things," and then try to stop him doing them. You prefer Smith to Jones, and then nag him to be more like Jones. You're like craftsmen who are always working with the wrong material, cabinetmakers who settle down in an iron foundry. Time and place never fit in with your desires. If there's no food for miles and hours, then you're hungry. Take you to a loaded dinner table, and your appetite's gone. If you find yourself in a bedroom with your lover, after oysters and champagne, you're not in a mood for making love; but let him take you to a committee meeting, a theater, or share with you a

27

crowded railway compartment, and you're suddenly seized with the wildest desires. You'll worry the best man you know, to make him better still, yet offer everything you have to the first cad who comes along. You dislike a bad-tempered man, and despise one who isn't. If a husband's idle and won't make money for you, he's a disgrace; but if he works hard to spend money on you, he's a fool. Whatever he is or does, he's always wrong and you're always right. But you don't even know what you're right about. You guard a fortress that isn't there.

NINA

And so you don't like us.

MATTHEW

My dear, I adore you.

STUART

Coward, coward, you daren't say anything else. But I dare—and do. As persons I can tolerate you both, but as members of your sex—and this specially applies to you, Nina—I regard you with detestation, alternating rapidly, bewilderingly, between contempt and horror.

NINA

Thank you, Stuart. Now I know how you feel, what a deep pleasure it must have been for you to be on this boat in my company for so long! Clearly you've been accepting hospitality, with some appearance of enjoyment too, from a brainless parasite, a creature who threatens to bite into your roots, to suck your blood, then cast enormous soft arms about you and drag your heaven-sent masculine genius down into the stifling body of the earth—that earth which has never been good enough for you even to walk upon. And how surprised some intelligent creature from another planet would be, after looking at and listening to your sex and mine, after learning what our respective functions are, to discover from you your vast superiority!

HARRIET

And then you must both remember that every luckless girl child is born into a society that men have made to suit themselves; a male society in which it is taken for granted that our feminine values are worth very little, and yours to be sought at all costs. For over two thousand years we women have been like the inhabitants of a conquered country, in which you men are the army of occupation—exacting tribute, banishing our customs, mocking at our ancient loyalties, debauching our currency, and at the least sign of protest sending your artillery and tanks rolling heavily through our streets. Remember we live in your society, not in our own.

NINA

And by now I think this society of yours is even worse than it outwardly appears. Although in the mass you are still ruling, individually you are beginning to lose your force. It is possible to submit, in every sense of the term, to bearded nomad chiefs, to warrior lords, to men who live in danger—but how about businessmen and civil servants sitting in offices, plied with cups of tea and altogether living far more tamely than the women themselves? Yours is like a tottering empire

29

where the Moguls are still on the throne, but their robes, their symbols of office, disguise dry bones. How can we creatures of flesh and blood flourish in such a world as that?

HARRIET

How can any creatures flourish in it? You destroyed the fine fat images of the Mother-Goddesses, put an end to their fertile, peaceful, comfortable dominion, to set up the image of the Father-God with his rationality and insistence upon order, his iron hierarchies, his theologians and judges and inquisitors, who have glared at us for twenty-five centuries. But where now is this reign of reason, this triumph of the conscious mind, this impersonal justice, this ordered progress of the intellect, when the very earth is raped and ruined and the masses of men upon it move like mindless sleepwalkers? It is not only that you have lost happiness: you have lost even the most elementary sense of safety. You say we would drag you back to the Cave. But you may soon be glad to be running into caves, those of you who are left after your mad hatred of life and idiotic pride have exploded in your faces.

STUART

Ladies—ladies—too much dubious anthropology, too much rhetoric. So, like Nina a few minutes ago, I'm not impressed. Come—you pretend to be the realists. Where are your plain home truths?

NINA

Here. Let me say what I think about men, the ordinary men who have inherited power over women and over the world. I have loved men. They have given

30

me much—though not all—of the joy I've known. You
see, even here, Stuart, I'm more generous than you are.
Yes, much joy. A man's hand revealing to me the shape
of my cheekbone through the plump covering of flesh;
desire with its queer pains and the extraordinary
worlds where you transport us in assuaging them; the
lazy intimacy of bodies; the intensity of words whis-
pered in emotion that bite into the memory and are
held forever: these are luxuries designed for gods, far
beyond commerce. Also, if men have taught me
nothing, they have enabled me to learn most of what I
know. And, unlike you, I'm not ungrateful, not too
proud to admit the debt. But now I wish merely to say
that I've discovered men in general to be dishonest in
thought, clever traitors to their own souls, pompous
and egotistical almost beyond belief, vain—mistaking
pique for sensitiveness—and brimming with a loath-
some mixture of complacency and self-pity. It's their
dishonesty that is the hardest for us to bear. I love a
man. I say something to him with direct human feeling, something that comes quite simply from the heart.
I expect a response from another human being, from
the sort of dear natural creature I have sometimes met
in the arms of love. But no. The man rushes up all
kinds of mental screens and reservations until he looks
to me like a henhouse elaborately camouflaged against
shellfire. He doesn't allow himself a true instinctive
response to what I've expressed, rejects the simple
reply from the heart, and turns himself into a moralist,
or a philosopher, or a man of wit and fashion; or only
allows himself a reply proper to an English gentleman,
a logical Frenchman, a bluff American, an exquisite
cosmopolitan—whatever form this idiotic impersona-

31

tion may take. And this to us is sacrilege. You cannot think with what terrible boredom, with what despair, we turn away, repulsed by this false façade of words, these lies in the soul.

STUART

And is that all—the best that you can do?

MATTHEW

It's quite enough for me.

NINA

Enough? All? We haven't even begun yet on your wooden insensitiveness, your childish egoism. Harriet?

HARRIET

Yes, it's that cast-iron male egoism which still astonishes me, depresses me, finally defeats me. When any woman is unfortunate enough to possess something like it, she goes into history as a monster. You have selves that extend to all parts of the horizon and fill the sky. And anybody belonging to you isn't really another person but merely an extension of your own ego. My father felt that he was devoted to my mother. He was a very busy man, but now and again he'd take a few days off, just for her sake, he said. And where did they go every time? To wherever there was a chess tournament. Women can be selfish of course, but at least they generally know when they're being selfish, whereas a man can be a monster of selfishness and yet imagine that he's sacrificing himself day and night. As for the man who is determined to be kind—there is no greater tyrant on earth. How often do you take a cool level look at yourselves, to see what's missing or what might be improved? Yet that is what women never stop doing, only to be jeered at for what is really their humility, their absence of conceit, their tenacious will to make themselves more desirable to men who may not think them worth ten minutes' trouble. We're always being accused of preferring bad men to good men, but the truth is that most of the so-called good men are even more self-centered and thick-skinned and delighted with themselves than the rascals are.

STUART

I like to consider myself just good enough for God, just bad enough for woman.

NINA

Fiddle-de-dee! But oh—the pompousness, the pomposity, of the male! I can see it. It's a small man with thin legs carrying an enormous paunch of self-importance. The little fellow himself is only just visible above and below his corporation.

MATTHEW (*with marked rhythm*)

On his own tum, he beats a drum, of pom-pom-positee!

STUART

Good God!

NINA

Darling, I love you most when you're silly.

STUART

Stop that. You're attacking our sex, not cooing with it.

33

HARRIET

I spend half my working life with pompous men, who clear their throats as if they were Cromwell clearing the House of Commons. But to me the wooden men are even more trying, if only because they're so much less vulnerable. There are two kinds of wooden men. The first kind are made of solid teak and weigh tons, and never listen to anything you say and, if you don't get out of their way, they just come rolling on and knock you down, without even knowing they're doing it. But much worse are the other kind, the very polite wooden men, who have been wound up to elaborate good manners in early youth and simply can't be stopped.

NINA

I knew one. He was so polite he used to hit me on the shins with his stick to make me walk inside him on the pavement.

HARRIET

I mean the kind of man who upsets half a drawing room, perhaps ruining a party, to open the door for me when I want to slip out quietly.

NINA

Oh yes—the one who tells us how well you're looking when you're near death, or is sorry you're feeling so tired when you're full of energy. And when these varnished pitch-pine robots are in love, they're worse still. They notice too much, exaggerating all the wrong things, until you feel you're living under a microscope and the very pores of your skin are like steaming pits.

MATTHEW

Poor Nina! It must be terrible to be dependent on such monsters.

NINA

But then I'm not dependent on them, Matthew darling.

STUART

You're about as independent of us as a bird is of the air, a man of his clothes, a meteorologist of the weather.

NINA

I can well imagine how you make that mistake. But you're quite wrong. I live through my senses—and live very well. Not one of you really understands what that means—you're all too cluttered up.

STUART

Not me. These other two are, no doubt.

NINA

No, you as well, Stuart. I'm quite different from you. I don't savor the world with exquisite detachment. I'm involved myself, just as much as God would be if He made the world.

STUART

It's been suggested He did.

NINA

I don't know. I've never felt quite sure. But if He did, then I've a fellow feeling for Him—or why shouldn't I say Her, just to show my neutrality. I can't generalize about my kind of experience, and won't, because my whole belief is in the particular. So instead I'll try to describe one afternoon. It was years ago—before I met you, Matthew—but I can still recall every sight, sound and smell of it, every touch. I was staying in the South of France with some friends. They had a villa with a private beach. The usual Riviera thing, you know, a curved sandy bay between two promontories with pine trees behind. All quite small and very delicious. This particular afternoon, in the hottest weather, I had stayed at home when the others went motoring, and I was lying under one of those huge umbrellas on the loose, soft sand above the beach. The umbrella was green and white with a fringe, and I was staring up enjoying the way it looked against the sky, when quite suddenly a seagull made a dash at it—or at me, I don't know which—and for a second hung there just above my head, pulling itself out of the dive. Its legs were drawn back against the body, flexed hard, and its wings pressed against the air so that they were fanned out toward the tip and I could see every feather, every barb of every feather. Its eyes were pale and fierce and utterly without thought; its bill was wide open—screaming. I felt as though I had been assaulted, as though a steel dart had been thrown into the very center of all my nerves and senses. In a way it was agonizing. My tongue knew what it was to be the tongue in that bird's hard, narrow bill, and my muscles shared in the pull on its wings and yellow legs. Of course it only lasted an instant, leaving me with a sharp aerial image of a woman in a bathing dress lying under a green and white umbrella. Then everything in the bay, in my domain of the moment, seemed to clamor for attention. The smell of the sea, the smell of the pine resin and the last traces of the scent I had forgotten I was wearing were suddenly strong in my nose. The sea and sky were extraordinarily brilliant, and the pine woods dark. I could hear the grasshoppers sawing away in the marram grass and imagined I could see the spread of their wings—light red and blue. Pine cones were popping in the heat like firecrackers. The warm sand felt wonderful to my fingers, and as I let it fall, through a chink, into a sliding cone close to my eyes, I saw how every speck had its own shape and was a fragment of something in the world—of a shell, or a lobster, or a vein of quartz, or a rock. As I watched them trickle down, these specks of sand, I saw rather than thought how some were quite new-made, bits of creatures alive in my own lifetime, while others were hundreds, thousands, millions of years old. I lay there a long while; I can remember how the shadow of the umbrella moved round on the sand. Then I heard the car coming up the drive, and I walked back through the wood, feeling the little bars of the pine needles under my bare feet, then the smooth marble slabs of the terrace. They gave me a Martini, a beautiful big dry one, and as it ran icily down my throat I felt a great joy and pride in belonging to a species that had lived long and cleverly enough to have perfected a Martini. The whole dome of the clear evening sky seemed to be the lining of my own skull. It was very odd—and exalted—never, never to be forgotten.

STUART

A glimpse inside the Cave at last. I'd no idea it would be so attractive.

HARRIET

I don't think it is. Oh yes—for one special occasion. But we have our everyday lives to live—

NINA

But experiences like that come every day—not so intense, it's true, but enough to keep me happy. I may have one when I wake and hear the wheels of the cart delivering the morning milk, or when I brush my hair, or lie in the bath admiring my body while the steam rises into the early sunshine. I may have one when I first step out of doors, or when I see a fruit stall or a pile of beautiful stuffs, or when Matthew gives me roses. There's no end to it, really.

STUART

I wonder? Aren't these sensations blunted as you grow older?

HARRIET

They must be. It's a child's world, a child's outlook.

NINA

No, it isn't. You don't understand. Even when "age has made me hideous," as you put it, Stuart, I shall still have fresh, stinging sensations. I shall probably have a very good idea of the texture of the inside of my coffin lid.

STUART (*very sharply*)

Don't talk like that. Not here and now.

NINA

Oh—I'm sorry, Stuart. I didn't realize—

HARRIET (*cutting in*)

But how much do they amount to, these private sensations of yours? What use are they to anybody?

NINA

No use—except to myself. And perhaps to God, who is helped in creating the world—

HARRIET

I consider that really blasphemous—and I don't believe I've ever said that before to anybody.

MATTHEW

Just a minute! I thought I heard Porson calling me.

(*He turns and goes off. The other three are motionless, listening. In the silence that follows we hear the distant sound of a steamer hooting, a lonely melancholy noise. Silence again.*)

NINA (*very softly, slowly*)

Only a minute ago . . . we were gigantic . . . reaching to the sky . . . filling the night . . . with our ideas and opinions . . . the colored lights of our temperament. Now, hit by a secret thought, how we have dwindled. The sky is no longer our roof, but a terrifying vacancy, hostile with all those glittering, alien worlds. How enormous the night seems . . . the eye of the moon is even smaller, colder, more inquisitorial than before. Look at those fishermen . . . their boat shows black as it crosses the path of the moon.

HARRIET

They are not very far away but they know nothing

of our troubles. They are shining a lamp down into the water to lure the fish.

STUART

Soon their nets will close on an unlucky few among all those hidden shoals. I believe the moon is our lamp . . . treacherous.

NINA

Yet how lovely it is. Jupiter there is low and bright enough to have his own trembling pathway on the water . . . not far from the moon's. I believe I can hear singing . . . very faintly . . . and I can still smell something fragrant, sensible, human, in the breeze. . . . Isn't it vanilla? How right it would be if the last thing one smelt was vanilla . . . and that's what I think it is . . . one's old nursery favorite—for chocolate, ice cream, sauces—dear vanilla—bless you! . . . .

(*They wait a moment, then turn.* MATTHEW *comes back, very much the owner of the yacht, the man of affairs.*)

MATTHEW

No news. Porson wasn't calling me. I've told him now to beat his dinner gong if any news comes through and we're wanted. Sorry to interrupt you like that. Carry on.

HARRIET

Nina, I don't like your attitude toward life. In fact, I hate it.

NINA

I thought you would.

40

HARRIET

I want to be fair. I realize there are times when I've been envious and jealous of you.

MATTHEW

Harriet, of course you haven't.

NINA

Don't be absurd—of course she has. I always expect envy and jealousy from my women friends, and I'm disappointed if they show no signs of them. In fact, I begin to wonder what they're up to.

MATTHEW

Why, what could they be up to?

NINA

Don't be silly, Matthew. Women are always up to something.

HARRIET

I merely wanted Nina to understand that tonight there isn't the least glimmer of envy and jealousy in my mind. It's the wrong night for that.

NINA

We're in the Dragon's Mouth.

HARRIET

Wherever we are, whatever's in store for us, I don't feel this is a time for striking affected attitudes.

NINA

Neither do I. I meant everything I said. I was asking

41

myself, before I spoke, what I lived for, and then I tried honestly to tell you.

HARRIET

You think I'm going to be dishonest?

NINA

Darling, I think you might pretend a little—oh, not for yourself, all in the way of duty, for the public good —to be *rather* grander and nobler than you actually feel when you're very much by yourself, when it's late and you ought to be asleep and the night's very long, very big, very cold—

MATTHEW

Nina, that's not Harriet. You ought to understand that by now.

NINA

What I do understand, my darling, is that she's your conscience, just as I—let us hope—am your joy. Perhaps in a perfect world we'd be one woman, specially for you. So you can see at a glance how imperfect this world is. But I accept it, cracked and flawed as it is, much better than you three do.

HARRIET

No, you don't, Nina. You don't accept it at all. You merely visit it at certain moments, as you've told us. You're a ghost that happens to have vivid and memorable sensations. You're so many unthinking nerve ends, just as Stuart is a razor-sharp intelligence cutting about it in a darkness of despair, and Matthew is simply a giant boy hurling himself into pursuits that are really boys' games to him—

MATTHEW

No, never!

NINA

And *I* say *No.*

STUART

I could say it too, but as there's justice in me as well as this darkness of despair, I merely say, "It's her turn now and not our place to interrupt." Go on, Harriet.

HARRIET

You people—Nina especially—talk as if you were alone in the world, as if you'd done everything for yourselves. You stand on a million shoulders to describe the view, then ask me to observe—and admire—your height and keen eyesight. You forget you've done hardly anything for yourselves. You wouldn't enjoy your fine perceptions, your exquisite sensations, if uncounted numbers of other people, to whom you never give a thought, hadn't lived before you, weren't still toiling and suffering all round you. Where's your gratitude? Where—even—your common decency? Not one of you would dream of staying at a hotel and then hurrying out early one morning to avoid paying the bill. Not one of you would accept a meal, or even a drink, from a friend without saying "Thank you." But to the great human society that has boarded and lodged you, has taught you almost everything you know, what have you done? Turned a blank face, without even a thought of gratitude. Yes, Matthew, even you. And Nina and Stuart are worse. For they make such a parade of their sensitiveness, the delicacy of their perceptions, their remoteness from the vulgar sweaty crowd, the mob, the common herd.

STUART

Harriet, there might be a soapbox somewhere on board—

MATTHEW

I thought you weren't going to interrupt.

STUART

I'm trying to help.

HARRIET

No, you aren't, damn your eyes! Well, I'm sorry if I was beginning to sound like a street-corner orator. Though I'm not sure I don't prefer street-corner orators, bellowing on their soapboxes, to aesthetes who understand nothing but their own exquisite sensations, who take and take and take without offering anything in return. Oh yes—no doubt I sound like a prig—

NINA

Well, darling, perhaps—just a little—

HARRIET

Perhaps I am a *prig*. I've been called one before now. I've been called a lot of things. That happens to women who've deliberately chosen to work in a man's world, women who hope to bring into that world all the feminine values it needs so badly. To work with men, meeting them fairly and squarely on their own territory, not using any of the blackmailing tricks of sex, and yet to remain a woman, with a woman's sense

44

of responsibility for persons, this seems to me the hardest but the best task on earth. I don't say I've succeeded in it—perhaps I've often been too weak and foolish—but I'm proud to have attempted it. And at least I've not remained a child, bent on my own pleasure, but have tried to pay my debt to the community.

MATTHEW

Yes, my dear Harriet, I think you have. I know what you feel, even if these two don't. But let me tell you now—as I've hinted more than once when we've been working together—you attempt too much. You do a good job, but you'd do a better if you'd take it easy now and again, if you didn't try so hard all the time, if you didn't treat an industrial problem as if it were a sick child and you were its mother.

STUART

But she feels she *is* its mother. How ungrateful you are, Matthew! She puts her gigantic maternal instinct to work for your company, cherishing your oil tanks and pipelines, canteens and ledgers, on her very bosom, and you tell her she's too conscientious. Of course she is, but—

MATTHEW

That's better than staring at first editions, broken pottery and the pussy cat, wondering if you've enough energy to write another sentence, probably about a world that's ceased to exist.

STUART

It hasn't ceased to exist in my mind—and the minds of a few other civilized persons—

45

NINA

And I hope you consider me one of them, Stuart, because I'm entirely with you. Is it our fault if Harriet finds herself suffocating in an air that no real woman could breathe—and still live?

HARRIET

I never suggested I was suffocating. I meant in fact to suggest that it's I who live to the full, struggling with the real world, helping persons, whereas people like you and Stuart are little better than ghosts. You've never grown up to accept responsibility. And you make so much of your little pleasures—an evening by a study fire, a hot afternoon on the seashore—all with a rather defiant air, because you know in your hearts you've never taken your share of adult responsibility. In the last resort, you're absentees, truants, shirkers.

MATTHEW

Bravo, Harriet! *Go hang yourself, brave Crillon! We fought at Arques and you were not there!*

NINA

Oh—don't talk rubbish, Harriet. I have the responsibility of Matthew's happiness—

HARRIET (*cutting in*)

Who told you he was happy?

MATTHEW

Just leave my happiness alone, the pair of you. Neither of you understands what gives me my own kind of joy nor what my life is really like. Nor do you,

46

Stuart. Here I must lump you with the women, my dear fellow.

STUART

And for once I prefer to be lumped with them. Not because I don't understand the sort of existence you lead, but because I don't understand how you can consent to lead it. In my view, it isn't a life but merely a one-man relay race, in which you dash at full speed round the track, hand yourself whatever it is that relay racers hand each other, and then go careering on again, your lungs bursting, your sight a red haze, only in the end to win a prize you don't want and which indeed you've had to award yourself. With the result that you're the richest man I know—and the poorest. And let me add, being fond of you, I say this regretfully.

MATTHEW

If you imagine that's a regretful tone, Stuart, you should buy one of those recording machines and try listening to yourself.

HARRIET

Useless! He's always listening to himself.

NINA

But what Stuart said was partly true. Matthew is worse than any woman in his attitude toward Time. He won't realize that Time, bringing the present moment and with it all our real contact with this delightful world, is our chief friend. Matthew treats it as an enemy. He shovels the weeks and months into the furnace of his impatience and dissatisfaction, like rub-

47

bish that must be burnt. Ever since I've known him he's behaved as if he felt that life would really begin five weeks on Tuesday.

HARRIET

Because, as I told you, he's simply a magnified boy. Yes, Matthew, in your own way, you're no more a responsible adult than they are. All your force, your formidable power, comes from your refusal to grow up, so that you've kept and even heightened a boy's wild tearing energy, ruthless impatience, contempt for the sober adult patterns of living. Many a time at a directors' meeting, when you've been in your glory, hastily sketching some new project, brushing aside all opposition, sweeping every timid objection into the wastepaper basket, you've made me remember my two brothers home for the holidays, first roaming hungrily round the house crying, "What shall we do?" and then plunging into some solemn boys' nonsense and refusing to do anything else, hardly recognizing anybody else's existence.

MATTHEW

Have you anything else to say, any of you, before counsel for the defense of this idiotic relay racer, this shoveler away of Time, this arrested adolescent, rises to address the Court? And let me remind you that so far I've said very little and have been an uncommonly good listener, while the three of you explained at length your highly superior attitudes toward life, your mastery of the art of living, all very different but all alike in being much better than anything I could imagine.

STUART

Matthew, your armor is pierced, if I may say so. You sound to me like a man about to lose his temper—

MATTHEW

Yes, I'm on the edge of it. Not because I've had to do so much listening and have done so little talking, although that's unusual. But because each of your three last speeches, putting me in my lowly place, was just one too many. And now it's my turn and don't let anybody try to stop me.

NINA

Darling, we wouldn't dream of it. Harriet and I adore you, and Stuart's frightened of you. So it's all yours.

MATTHEW

Thank you, my dear. Well, let me tell you first that all three of you are babies. Oh—very fancy babies, I grant you, with special perceptions, exquisite sensations, maternal longings, but nevertheless, in the real world that I understand, just babies. Like babies, you have to accept what you find about you, what the world offers you, and make the best of it, as you've all so elaborately explained. Not one of you changes anything, makes something new, becomes a creator. But Man, essential Man, the creature in the image of God, is the changer, the maker, the creator. As somebody —was it Paracelsus?—said—"God placed Man in an imperfect world so that Man should make it perfect." And I am that Man, no doubt a poor specimen of him, but a true Man in that sense. You accept the world

49

and this life, but I change them. And there is my happiness, the joy that you can never find. It never lasts long; for the curious groping mind, occasionally flashing forward, the desire to change, make, create, the hunger of the heart, are only satisfied for a moment; but there is more depth, more value, in their very dissatisfaction than in all your passive enjoyment. Not being stupid and vulgar, not one of you accused me of sacrificing my life for mere money. And I owe nothing to any political-economic system, as so many fools think, because men like me succeed to power under any system, not because it is power we want—

STUART

Are you sure, my friend, are you sure?

MATTHEW

No, I am not, my friend. But what I *am* sure of is that behind my own drive for power is that hunger of the heart for a nobler earth, that restless search for something new and better which is not a human weakness but a divine command. There are men—and I do business with many of them—who work hard because they are too dull to do anything else. But I challenge any of you to declare that I am one of these desiccated slaves of the machine. Never have I resented other people's pleasures—didn't I tell you how much Nina's happiness lighted my life? But if I turn aside, drop the game, quit the party at its height, it is because there is so little time, so much to do, so few who will steel themselves to do it. Yes, I have driven men, ruthlessly at times, because most men have to be driven, to be saved from their own indolence and in-

50

difference and cowardice, so that the life they dream of idly can be realized on this earth. There must be conflict, too. Without conflict, without opposition, there is no creation. We run great risks, and compel other men to share those risks, but without such ventures into the dark and onto the uncharted sea, never undertaken without some one man's directed energy and heightened will, we should still be so many apes, muttering and scratching, at the mercy of any passing flood or drought.

STUART

What we are at the mercy of now is worse than any passing flood or drought—thanks to you formidable creative men, whose next creation looks like being the engine of total destruction.

NINA

And I would rather be an ape, or any jungle creature, than most of your baffled modern men in their air-conditioned offices and with their word-conditioned minds, shut off from the sun and every living thing.

HARRIET

And Matthew, men like you do what you want to do, harnessing and directing your energy and heightening and hardening your will, not out of service, not out of love, but because you cannot live in any other fashion.

MATTHEW

All this is the whining of cowards; the blind clinging to what is safely known; the old refusal to leave the forest to till the soil, to put out to sea to find new continents; the fear of the plough, the wheel, the sword, the chariot, the sail, the engine, the flying machine. I tell you we are here to master the earth and not to come to idle easy terms with it. Man is either the changer, the maker, the creator, or he is nothing—an animal shivering in the wind. And either we mold this earth to our will, changing its very climates to suit our needs, or we shall be merely another of its bewildered wretched creatures, and perhaps the worst of them, knowing we are doomed. There is the battle—dwarfing all the battles that are merely the accidents of our time—and I would rather die in it than live a thousand years of pleasure and ease. I may be all that you said I am—and indeed much worse, for there are things you might have said you did not say—but I fight in that battle while one of you, Harriet, joins us reluctantly, deploring the very will that gives us victory, and the other two of you ask to be admired for loitering over the spoils of old campaigns. If as you say I seem to be running a madman's race, it is because those who can catch a glimpse of the future must run ahead of those who see nothing. If as you say I treat Time as my enemy, it is because I know his moments fly so fast and that they must be filled with creation before they are lost forever. If as you say I appear to be an overgrown boy let loose and wild with energy, that is because I feel that to grow old and cautious and tired is to accept defeat. Oh yes—I have a thousand faults, but if I had ten thousand more I would still be beyond the final damnation of any criticism of yours, because I am Man the Maker. We are not those who do three men's work so that we can retire to some warm island and grow sleek in the sun, or because the days are so long before the undertaker calls. We are those who know that now men have no choice except between the end of our species as anything but a decaying animal, and the final fulfillment of the creature that heard God's command to be dissatisfied, to continue His task of creation, to make the morning's work serve the dream in the night, to arrive at complete mastery of this earth. I tell you, we are—

(*but he is interrupted by the sound of the gong, a deep, hollow and frightening sound. They listen intently, all rigid*).

STUART

There's always one last ironic voice in every debate. I think we've just heard it.

NINA

For a moment it stopped my heart.

MATTHEW

I'm sorry, my dear. It means that a message is coming through. Perhaps you'd all like to come down with me. Anyhow, I think we need a drink.

NINA

Darling, I'm sure we do. Come on, Harriet. My dear, you're shivering. Matthew, a drink—a drink!

(*They all turn*—NINA has a hand on HARRIET's arm —*and go out. Lights change.*)

PART TWO

(*After the house lights go down, there is a moment's darkness or dimness, then the spots come on, and* NINA *and* HARRIET *enter and come forward. They might now wear light or short coats. They speak in a tone we have not heard from them before, a quiet confidential tone, that of women who know they are in a crisis but are not rattled.*)

NINA (*enjoying the fresh air*)

This is better. I couldn't have stayed any longer below. Did you notice Stuart—his hands and lips?

HARRIET

Yes. He's desperately overwrought. We all are, but I'm not surprised he takes it the hardest.

NINA

That's because you don't like him. We always expect our men, the men we like, to be calmly courageous, masters of the situation, while the rest are helpless, waiting to be saved.

HARRIET

I don't doubt Stuart has as much courage as the rest of us. It's only that this situation—and Heaven knows it's ghastly enough for anybody—is the worst possible

55

situation for him to endure. His intellect tortures him because there's nothing for it to do. He hates the confusion of uncertainty, the contact with physical horrors, while all the feelings he never expresses begin to rise in great waves, pounding his defenses.

NINA

This must be a situation much harder for any man to bear—just waiting for bad news. Women have always been waiting for bad news. Matthew is extraordinary. Perhaps he's exercising his power to cut off his imagination, which is something Stuart can't and won't do. But anyway he's wonderfully reassuring, it is Matthew who is keeping us on our feet.

HARRIET

Of course. Matthew has great courage.

NINA

More than I could have believed. But what I'm wondering now is whether I've enough fortitude to see me through—either as hostess to a plague party or of course as prospective victim.

HARRIET

You won't be the one who's infected. I'm certain of that.

NINA

My dear, that's absurd. How can you be certain?

HARRIET

Because—in spite of all the education that's been stuffed into me—I believe in luck. And I know—*I know*—you're one of the lucky people, Nina. Things like that just don't happen to you. Now Stuart—or—me—

NINA (*who has heard Stuart's approach*)

Sh! He's here.

(STUART *arrives. He is feeling the strain, and although he tries hard to be the man we met in Part One, he can't quite manage it.*)

What's happened, Stuart?

STUART

Nothing. They're still fiddling about with the radio set. And I couldn't stay in there any longer—watching them, feeling helpless—

HARRIET

What's wrong with the set?

STUART

God knows! Or does He?

NINA

I doubt it. All those switches and valves and electrical gadgets, you can be certain, belong to the Devil. Hell is probably crammed with the most astonishing machinery and clever devices, like a submarine a million miles long.

STUART

If you're not right, Nina, you ought to be. And notice how, with truly hellish malice, the machine breaks down just when you need it most. A voice tells us that the blood tests clearly prove that three of us are all right but the fourth is definitely infected and must be removed as soon as possible. And then—nothing—nothing. The damnable instrument splutters and fades, and now won't release another word. And that's all we want—a single name, that's all—but we have to wait.

NINA

I don't think I'm sorry not to know yet.

STUART

I don't believe you. It's an intolerable suspense.

NINA

Then we must try to make it tolerable. We've been allowed a little grace.

(MATTHEW *arrives, bustling a little. He is wiping his brow, not out of anxiety but because he is hot.*)

MATTHEW

You were quite right not to stay. It's damnably hot in that little radio room. Porson's soaked through and has had to strip.

STUART

Is he stripping that infernal set of his?

MATTHEW

He's doing that too. I don't understand what's wrong—for Porson, like most minor experts, likes to make a mystery of his job—but apparently it'll take him some time to put it right. So there it is. I'm sorry, Nina—Harriet—but we can't tell you any more. One of us has got the horrible thing, but we don't know which one. There's a motorboat on its way out to us. I know, not a pleasant thought, and I'm sorry I men-

58

tioned it. However, the odds are heavily in favor of my having caught the infection. It started among the crew, and I'm the only one of us who spends any time with the crew. So it's ten to one in favor of my being infected.

STUART

It would be if we lived in a reasonable corner of the universe. But we don't. We live in a world where some ruffian who's spent his life with pox, fever and plague dies in his sleep at the age of ninety, and a child who's been kept from all contamination goes down with polio during her sixth birthday party.

NINA

That's true, but I don't think you need to be so bitter about it. If we'd lived in what seemed to us a completely reasonable world, where the terrible unexpected never happened, we'd have become extinct from sheer boredom ages ago.

HARRIET

Yes, all depth of feeling would have vanished.

MATTHEW

And there'd have been nothing large and vital for us to do, nothing to put right, nothing to challenge our skill and invention and fellow feeling. We'd have all felt as empty and desiccated as those sad old monkey-faced people who go drearily round and round the world on luxury cruises.

NINA

With life a perpetual Captain's Dinner, and all of us desperate in our colored paper hats. But I agree with

Stuart that just because Matthew gave himself the best chance of being struck down, it doesn't follow that the chance will have been taken. On the other hand, he's the most useful of us, and this Unseen Assassin has a fancy for knifing useful people just as he has for attacking the most promising children. So the odds are about even. But if it's me—and perhaps it ought to be—I can only hope everything happens quickly. It's not the end but the approach to the end that terrifies me. For that's where those moments of mine can be so treacherous. They can swell out enormously for pain and terror as well as for happiness. All this talk of things happening "instantaneously"— it's such nonsense. Time can seem to stand still. I remember when that plane to Stockholm turned over—I suppose the pilot only lost control of it for a second or so—and we were all flung about and everything that could be broken seemed to be breaking. Within three seconds, a few ticks of the clock, we were getting back into our seats, feeling our cuts and bruises. Nevertheless, those three seconds were like a long visit to some horrifying place; I can remember thinking quite slowly, "In another moment this plane will be on fire and I'll be fried alive. And what's *that* going to be like?" I didn't see the whole of my previous life, but there seemed quite enough time for it. And think what happens when you go under or come out of an anesthetic. Instantaneous? All over in a flash? Never! Why, they're like trips to and from the moon.

MATTHEW

It was the same when I was in that motor smash. Everything went into the most appalling slow motion

60

once the accident was happening. Although you just hadn't time to *control* anything, you'd all the time in the world to notice everything that was happening. As if time had split into two—a fast one for action and a slow one for observation and feeling. A nightmare atmosphere.

HARRIET

But *was* it a nightmare atmosphere, Matthew? Because I would have thought it was the very opposite. In a nightmare you're completely possessed by fear—and indeed I suppose that Terror is the author, stage manager, scene designer and cast of the whole drama. A nightmare is, so to speak, all our irrational fears justifying themselves by staging a midnight performance. That's why it's much worse than anything we experience in waking life.

STUART

How do you know it is? There are a lot of things people have experienced in waking life, especially in this age of organized horror, that haven't yet come your way, Harriet. Prolonged torture. Starvation that reduces you to cannibalism. A slow decay into idiocy. And don't forget you've already told us, in a misguided effort to keep us cheerful, that the personality, the experiencing and tormented self, doesn't retreat altogether from these hells on earth, but is still there, imprisoned, despairing—

HARRIET

But I'm coming to that, if you'll only let me make my point. I agree with Nina and Matthew that in

61

moments of crisis, of danger at its height, time goes into slow motion so that every moment seems like five minutes of ordinary life. But something else happens too, which makes it quite different from a nightmare. I remember it very well from the morning during the war when our ship was torpedoed. Everything went into slow motion, with one fantastic event following another. But my real self, the experiencing, recording part of me, seemed quite detached from the events, as if I were merely watching a film of a ship being torpedoed. It made me feel—and I've never lost the feeling since—that nothing final and fatal could happen to the essential Me—

STUART

Yes, yes, yes, my dear Harriet—but don't delude yourself. That's a well-known phenomenon, out of which the preachers and theologians hasten to make capital; but any psychologist will tell you that that detachment is merely a defense mechanism of the mind coming into operation.

MATTHEW

And what have you said, when you've said that? In my opinion—nothing. What's a defense mechanism? We're not machines. And what good is served by pretending we are? If a man is crawling down a slippery deck trying to launch a boat, or is trying to remove the fuse from an unexploded bomb, and at that moment he feels detached from the danger he's in, feeling that he's an immortal soul out of reach of it, what's the use of telling him he's merely set up a defense mechanism? If there's one thing I'm sick of, living as I do in a world where men must take action to keep alive, it's these unending learned attacks on men's dignity, courage and self-respect. If we don't all behave like apes, it's not the fault of all our most recent and famous instructors. And I'm no scientist, philosopher, psychologist, scholar—I've had to educate myself late at night—but it seems to me all these fellows who tell us we're *nothing but* this, *only* that, *merely* the other, always contrive to leave themselves, their own lives and motives for living them, out of the picture. Darwin devotes his life to proving that we're what we are through blind adaptation to environment. And how does that explain Darwin? Marx scratches away in the British Museum, poor and proud, proving that we're completely conditioned by economic forces. And how does that explain Marx? Freud risks mockery and abuse and his professional reputation to tell us that we're at the mercy of the erotic pleasures of our infancy and that our rationality is so much elaborate self-delusion. And how does that explain Freud? The world is now full of fellows living in miserable back rooms on tinned beans so that they can devote themselves to proving that no man merely for the sake of an idea could possibly live in a miserable back room on tinned beans. Painters and writers risk starvation to produce pictures and books whose object is to show us that life is not worth living at all. This is an age in which most men who follow the dictates of their immortal souls do it only to tell us that we have no immortal souls. And millions and millions of ordinary people, who need some heartening faith to keep them going, just because they're not artists, scientists and philosophers, goaded on by an Idea, are beginning to

63

believe them, and if you want to know the conse-
quences, just look around you. So I say—to hell, where
it belongs, with your *defense mechanism*!

STUART

And I say—to the Devil, who owns it, with the idea
that we should cut down, soften and sweeten the truth
as we find it so that it may be acceptable to your millions of ordinary people who must have something to
keep them going. Let them work, eat, drink, sleep and
copulate, and for the rest obey the nearest parson,
priest, witch doctor or medicine man. If you are sick of
learned attacks on man's dignity, I am equally sick of
the pretense that in the mass he has any dignity. As I
want neither his vote nor his pennies, I can afford not
to join in this fuss over the Common Man. And if a
perfect egalitarian society were achieved tomorrow, I
should condemn it utterly—and cut my throat the day
after tomorrow. I simply do not believe that all our
hard-won resources should be poured out to keep millions and millions of plain folk in slightly better creature comforts—men and women with their trivial
virtues and trifling nastinesses, who in any case take
up most of the rope that is allowed them by their end-
less fecundity. And not because I think so little of
them, for indeed I have a far higher opinion of ordinary men and women than the sentimental dema-
gogues who cadge their votes and the newspaper
barons who corrupt their decency. I respect them
enormously as an indispensable part of an organic
whole. I want them to live as well as they can without
crippling those who might fulfill them through the
greatness of their gifts. Do roots envy the flowers—or

64

guts the lovely faces—that they nourish? But it is the very people you are ready to be so emotional about, the pampered mob that swarms everywhere now, demanding to know but never to learn, insisting upon art, science, philosophy and scholarship being minced, potted and spiced to please its disgusting palate, no more able to endure the naked truth than they can endure the sight of their naked bodies, who are destroying civilization and reducing us all to one beastly common denominator of mechanized barbarism. I don't keep a shop and have no customers to please, so don't ask me to water down and sweeten the truth because the mass has neither mind nor stomach for the facts of this life.

HARRIET

And that is sheer arrogance, Stuart. Since when were you so devoted to the truth? How many of the facts of our situation here, tonight, are you ready to face?

NINA

No, Harriet, that's not fair. Stuart, you needn't answer her.

STUART

Thank you, Nina, but I insist upon answering her. Here is the truth, here are the facts, about our situation, about myself; and I wonder which one of you dare follow my example. For look—now at last Death is confronting us in person. We are all born condemned to die: we accept that dictum, but how rarely our imagination lets the cat out of the bag for us, how seldom we allow ourselves to experience the reality of our death sentence! Just occasionally in the night it clutches us, makes us writhe in efforts to drive it back, to batten it down again in the dark holds of forgetfulness. Now within a few days one of us will be dead— yes, will have died horribly. But which of us will it be? Well, if there were sense and justice in such events, I know who ought to go. I should be the one. Yes, Harriet, the arrogant Stuart, whom you challenged to face the facts—I—I ought to go. And I say it, having dreadful knowledge of our end. I take it that none of us has the consolation of a belief in personal survival; none of us expects to meet on the shining pavements of an after life as Matthew and Harriet, Nina and Stuart?

(*He turns to the others, looking at them in turn. A pause.*)

To my ear your silence makes this announcement. It says that your minds, your intellects, have refused you this indulgence, but that secretly you keep alive a little hope, a little dog of hope kenneled somewhere in your emotions. He jumps and wags his tail when you call him. Isn't that the truth? Yes, it is true. Now I don't keep pets of that kind to console me. I am certain of my final and complete extinction when my heart ceases to beat.

HARRIET

You can't be certain. None of us can be. And even if we were, we can still believe that our individual lives contribute to something eternal—and in that sense *are* eternal.

STUART

Of course, of course. We have all had our faiths, sometimes bound in old calf, sometimes in limp leather. We can't have lived, struggling in our different ways, for so many years just for the sake of passing pleasures, or from the mere habit of keeping ourselves alive. I have had my own faith; references to it may even be found in printed works. But I know that I haven't served it well. I have never abandoned myself to life, never allowed it to blow through me, to transport me. That is why I ought to be the one to die. I have denied life not thrice, but always. I have believed in civilization, in exactness and mental self-discipline, in what is fine and hard, not soft and easy; but under it all I have known that these disciplines are of small worth without abounding energy, without fire. Five hundred million years have gone to raising the human brain from primeval ooze, and now already it is running to seed. Perhaps it needs the shadowy ooze, and now it is like a plant on parched ground. We clever men—and we hunt in small packs—who have no weight or authority, no simple feeling and, worst of all, no instincts and no inner darkness, we are becoming the curse of the world. Whether we are blameworthy, or whether we are as helpless in the grip of history as the poor dinosaurs, I don't know—only that we are a curse. Our brains are like sharp-bladed chaff machines, cutting smaller and smaller. If any fire lingers, then we quench it. I myself have never had the courage to fulfill my inmost desires. And already life takes its revenge, visiting me in my dreams clothed in its most shameful dress. I have never told you, have I, Matthew, that your scholarly, dandy friend Stuart enjoys dreams worthy of a pimp? What a hell that would be if we passed through the grave to enter the country of our dreams! Let me thank the Heaven that isn't there for my extinction. I tell you this prim arrogant brain of mine, this discreetly exercised, well-tended body, deserve the worm. Their fire has burnt so low that they have asked for the final cold.

NINA

No, Stuart, no! It isn't like that.

STUART

I will only say that it was not always so. Imagine me, if you can, when I was young and first went to the university, an excited boy. I had rooms in a famous medieval court. Many great men had lodged there through the centuries—scholars, philosophers and poets—and to me it seemed that every one of them was still in residence, that the lamps still burned in their old rooms. So I came to see all history as a time-less building, its windows lighted by generations of great men. Sometimes at night I would slip out into the court, sit by the rustling fountain, and tell myself stories of the lives of my predecessors. Soon these stories would turn into fantasies about myself. I was good-looking, clever and much praised. It was easy to grant myself a place among the immortals. I do not know at what step between winning his prizes at the university and being lowered into an undistinguished grave a man like myself accepts his failure. Certainly I accept mine tonight. Emotion, fear, give a wonderful clarity to one's vision; seem to give ordinary life the form of a work of art. So perhaps now for the first time I clearly accept my failure, but I have long recognized its face in secret. I have sat in my study and known not the exquisite enjoyments you credited me with, but a flat despair. I have asked myself where I went

68

wrong, what I lacked. I didn't want to move men and events like Matthew, but I have longed for his energy, for the imagination he has squandered, for his maddening ability to understand without taking thought. Surely with those gifts I could have achieved greatness. I have envied Nina her childlike freedom to enter into the real world, to be united with its loveliness, its physical zest. Had that been granted to me at least perhaps I could have been poet enough to wear a few shreds of immortality. But I have been myself, without energy, without fire in my imagination, without direct experience. I am poorer now than I was when I sat by the fountain. I have failed . . . but tonight failure itself has a shape. I do not abandon my ideal. I still believe that mankind is justified only by its great men, the creators whether famous or unknown. That is why I can envy in Harriet only some of her emotion, and why all she said earlier in criticism of us never touched me. For I have no desire for social and moral feeling. There is no morality and no progress in art or in pure thought; but their treasures accumulate so that each generation can be richer than the one before. Yes, I still believe in my timeless building, though I cannot have my room there. It still justifies life . . . and defeats death.

NINA

Dear Stuart, believe me when I say I never liked you better than I do at this moment.

MATTHEW

And let me add, my dear fellow, that I've often envied you in the past and that I envy you no less

now. You say you've failed—but—good God!—I'd
hate to hear a man like you tell me he'd succeeded in a
world like this. Energy and feeling and rich enjoyment
of the moment, all that you think you lack, are all very
well, and no doubt the rest of us can supply one or
other of them in full measure; but you've always had
a mind as clean and bright as polished steel, and many
a time when I've caught my reflection in it, I've seen
myself looking clumsy and ill-finished, and I've told
myself to live better, to take more trouble.

NINA

Stuart, that's true. You can believe him—he's often
said so.

STUART

But—don't you see—before tonight you'd never
catch me admitting envy or the least deficiency in myself. Now Matthew dwarfs and desiccates me again by
his very size and generosity. No, no, Matthew, I'm not
complaining. In fact—and you may guess how I hate
to admit it and how strange it is—I feel most deeply
moved.

HARRIET

It seems to me high time you were.

NINA

And I resent that, Harriet. Lord help us!—how un-
fair women like you can be! You've nothing more to
say than that—yet you were the challenger—defying
him to tell the truth, to face the facts of our situation
here. You make him strip himself to the bone yet still
keep your mind nipping him like an east wind.

70

Where's all the fine feeling, the tender social conscience, you boasted when you were lecturing us
before we went below, telling us we were so many
pleasure-loving children compared to you? Have people always to be at a distance, in nameless crowds,
before you feel for them? Does your charity always
begin far from home? Can't we at last qualify for your
sympathy? One of us must die—

HARRIET

I shall die.

(*They stare at her, shocked.*)

No, I don't feel ill, if that's what your looks are asking. I merely feel rather strange, a trifle lightheaded
perhaps, with everything outside myself beginning to
retreat and dwindle and lose reality, turning into the
landscape and furniture of a dream.

STUART

You're simply in the state we're all in, then. I take it,
none of us feels ill. But we know from what we saw
yesterday how suddenly and hard the disease strikes
at the end. It's as if one of us were loaded with a bomb
and already the fire is advancing swiftly along the fuse.
But we don't know who is holding it. So why the
dramatic announcement, Harriet?

HARRIET

I wasn't trying to startle you or to cut short Nina's
attack upon me. As she spoke, I felt it more strongly
than ever—that I'd be the one to go, that in some way
I can't explain the whole shape and pattern of our four
lives made it inevitable that I would be the one. I shall

71

die stupidly, blundering into it, just as I've lived stupidly.

MATTHEW

Harriet, my dear, you're not to talk like that. Nina may have been a little hard on you, just as you were on Stuart, but we don't expect—

HARRIET (*cutting in sharply*)

Nina was right. Who am I to challenge Stuart or anyone else, to talk of the truth and the facts of our situation here as if I owned them, to rant at and hector you as if I were an angry schoolmistress and you were so many children?

MATTHEW

I think we all took something of that tone. I know I did, telling you that you were so many babies. We tried to shout down our deep uneasiness, puffing ourselves up because we were secretly afraid. Now we know something we didn't know then. One of us talks for the last time.

NINA

Yes, and as we don't know which one, then all of us talk for the last time. Or keep quiet, which might be better.

HARRIET

Not for me, it wouldn't. And how can I be silent when I goaded Stuart into making his confession? Yes, Stuart, and I felt about it as they did, never admiring you more.

72

STUART

That's handsome, Harriet, though I fancy you could easily admire me more, never having admired me at all.

HARRIET

You're quite wrong. I've admired you—probably far more than Nina has—for years, always in spite of a large protesting part of myself. It's that part of course that told you it was high time you were genuinely moved. But it goes deeper than a mere rebuke. It links up with that admiration, reluctant on the surface but striking deep roots; and I am one of those women who when they admire a man are impatient for him to be perfect; but without deep feeling, even with so many gifts, you still fell short of what I wanted. And that is why I cried, "It seems to me high time you were." Of course it was a stupid cry—and Nina was quite right to turn on me—but then it was only one of a hundred thousand remarks, ill-timed, ill-chosen, that have dropped from my lips like the toads in the fairy tale— oh—for as long as I can remember. I'm one of those unlucky people of whom it's always said, "Her heart's in the right place," because nobody knows what the right place is—or cares. "Harriet means well," they always said, after I'd gone and they were glad to see me go.

MATTHEW

Harriet, this self-portrait seems to me completely false.

HARRIET

How can you tell—when I've never been anything but a blurred image in your mind? You've never yet taken one good long searching look at me. No, not even to say you didn't like what you saw. You take in more of Nina in one smiling glance than you've done of me in ten years' work together. Just a blurred image, that's all—like one of those beastly composite photographs—the modern Career Woman—so keen, so alert, so ambitious yet so deeply feminine in her broad sympathy. And I have to live behind this idiot mask—a woman, weeping invisible tears—helpless.

MATTHEW

But why should you feel like this? You've been unusually successful in your work; you've many good friends; you live well, travel a great deal. Yet now you're beginning to talk about yourself as if you were some half-starved, friendless creature drudging away in a back kitchen. And an hour ago you were denouncing the three of us for never giving a thought to all the people toiling and suffering all round us. My dear Harriet, why don't *you* give them a thought, compare your life with theirs, and then ask yourself if all this talk of weeping and helplessness is reasonable?

HARRIET

Of course it isn't reasonable. I wasn't being reasonable. For once I'm not *trying* to be reasonable. But of course I must go and offend even you, Matthew.

MATTHEW

Damn it—you're not offending me. But you mustn't tell me that I've never taken a good look at you, that you're only a blurred image in my mind, that you have to wear an idiotic mask. It's an insult to both of us.

74

I can't work with a woman for years, promoting her half a dozen times, and consider her one of my closest friends, without having a very clear picture of her capabilities, outlook and character. This blurred image you talk about is the one you have of yourself.

STUART

Of course you have the clearest picture of her capabilities, Matthew, of what value she has to you and your concerns, but that has nothing to do with what Harriet is trying to tell us. She could work closely with you for half a century but to the end you would still refuse to see anything that disturbed and broke the pattern of this working partnership, because you are entirely ruthless in your devotion to the tasks you set yourself.

MATTHEW

Certainly not. I know the kind of man you mean— I've had dealings with plenty of them—but I'm not that type at all. I consider other people, try to make all allowances—

STUART

But the rest of us don't *try* to make allowances. We *have* to make them, whether we wish to or not. But you're entirely ruthless. It's one of the things I most admire about you—that magnificent, uncompromising singleness of purpose. Because you know where you are going and what you want, in a world of doubt and indecision and confused vague longings, you can almost hypnotize the rest of us into obedience by a few words of command.

75

MATTHEW

My dear fellow, I never heard such nonsense. I might be able to galvanize a few technicians, clerks and foremen into brisk activity. I'd be ashamed of myself if I couldn't. But you're talking now as if the same thing applied to people like you and Nina and Harriet—

STUART

Of course I am. Because it does.

HARRIET

It never occurred to me that you didn't know.

MATTHEW

I still don't know. Now, Nina, you can't possibly agree with this, for you know how easy I am and how you do anything you please.

NINA

Anything that doesn't interfere with any plan of yours. No, darling, I'm not complaining. I'd hate to be married to any other sort of man. I must live with a man whose major plans are no more under my control than the weather. But of course they're right about you, Matthew my love. Always you drive us where you wish to go. Otherwise we shouldn't be here—oh how stupid!

STUART

I hope you wouldn't walk into that trap.

NINA

Sometimes I'm a fool and so talk like one.

76

MATTHEW

Now—wait a minute—you all wanted to come on this trip.

(*He looks at them. A pause.*)

STUART (*shrugging*)

Well, there's no help for it. I can't speak for Harriet—

HARRIET

She can speak for herself. No, Matthew, I didn't want to come on this trip. It was horribly inconvenient, getting away for so many weeks, and I hate the tropics, always have—I loathe the heat, the glare, the huge appalling waste of life.

NINA

I can enjoy that, but I dislike all the flavorless days at sea and—worse still—the rough weather when one lives in a reek of paint and bilge, with a headache and a sick taste—

STUART

I wouldn't accept this or any other yacht as a gift, if I had to use it. Moreover, I'd arranged to spend some time with Walters at the museum, and it won't be easy to persuade him to give me any other time. No, Matthew, like the women, I came reluctantly but swept along by the current of your will.

MATTHEW

All three! Well, I'll be damned!

(*He roars with laughter but then, as they don't join*

77

*him, clearly he suddenly remembers the situation
they are in and looks grave, conscience-stricken.*)

No—by Heaven—you're right. It isn't funny. I was
forgetting what had happened. Now it has to be me—
by God it does. I'll see what Porson's doing with that
set.

(*He turns and goes out briskly. There is a moment's
silence.*)

NINA (*after pause*)

How sweet he is. He was always the same. Stuart,
do you remember that morning in Paris when he first
carried me off?

STUART

Of course I do. It was just after the encounter with
the Turkish ambassador. I was trying to educate your
eye—I didn't know then that the easiest way is to
make violent love to a woman and then let the education seep through afterward—and that morning we
were finishing off the Louvre—

NINA (*taking in* HARRIET *now*)

And had arrived at one of the more obscure and
definitely morguelike rooms, while outside it was
spring; the Paris chestnuts were speaking of it with
the opening of their leaves—like small expressive
hands. It made me restive. A man who looked like an
attendant came hurrying in, and told Stuart he was
urgently wanted at the director's office. So off he went.
Then, there was Matthew—I'd only met him for a
moment a few days before—with that dancing gleam
in his eye. "They'll be hours and hours," he said, "and

78

it's a marvelous morning. I'll drive you up to Saint Germain and we'll have an early lunch on the terrace overlooking the whole city." And of course I went— that gleam in his eye was irresistible—and after a heavenly lunch up there, he told me he'd been following Stuart and me and had invented the message himself. And by that time, though I pretended to be cross, I didn't care—

STUART

Of course you didn't. No more educated-eye nonsense, no more culture for you. After that it was lunches, dinners, films and dancing with Matthew until you both flew home to get a marriage license. And I was left out in that cold where I may be said to have been, more or less, ever since. Not that I blame you, Nina. Most women would have done what you did.

NINA

I was caught up in the intense privacy and irresponsible high spirits of the first days of love. I remember how on that very night, or it might have been the next, Matthew had to break an engagement with some woman he knew quite well, so he rang her up and told her he was in a nursing home for observation and I chimed in—having had two champagne cocktails— and pretended to be a French nurse, telling the poor woman that Matthew mustn't tire himself with talking on the telephone. I've often wondered if I took her in.

HARRIET

Oh yes, Nina, she was completely deceived, even though she'd made a special journey to Paris to see

Matthew, partly on business, as of course he knew, but not altogether on business, as she knew very well. Yes, Stuart, I was the woman, left out in the cold like you, though I fancy it felt even colder where I was. And as you and I have the tidier minds, we ought to enjoy seeing the pattern so tidily finished off.

STUART

Strange as it may seem to you, my dear Harriet, I do. For when I say I relish irony, unlike most people I really mean what I say.

NINA

Oh—Harriet—I never realized it was you. So, for better or worse our lives have been intertwined for as long as that. . . . And now this sword is hanging over all four of us.

STUART

No—no—please—not *the sword.* How dishonestly we misuse words—corrupted by the politicians and the journalists! Always *the sword!* We must *unsheathe the sword.* That venerable weapon is whipped out by our tongues when we wish to refer to roasting peasants with napalm or pulverizing them with high explosive and hot steel. We shall soon all be atomizing one another with the Sword of Peace. And now you use this word to describe, or rather to conceal, some peculiarly horrifying microbes. For heaven's sake, Nina, be above that sort of thing. Chatter, chatter, by all means, but don't abuse language and our intelligence.

(MATTHEW *has now arrived.*)

Well, Matthew, what's the news?

MATTHEW

Porson thinks the motorboat will be here before he has the set working again. We know it's on its way.

STUART

Carrying Doomsday for one of us. An ugly visitation. But then I've always thought motorboats ugly things.

HARRIET

Please let me speak. While there is time and I have the heart for it, let me say something. For it was I who, when we were defending ourselves before, criticized all of you most bitterly, condemned you for not having taken your share of adult responsibility, called you absentees, truants, shirkers—

NINA

My dear, we were all finding unpleasant names for each other. What does it matter?

HARRIET

It matters to me. For I still believe that it will be I who will be taken away in that motorboat, that I will blunder into this miserable stupid death as I have gone blundering through life. So please—please let me speak. Yes, of course—I know what your silence is saying, what your looks say—for I have known that silence, those looks, so many times before—and they tell me I am being too emotional, that I am bringing more feeling to the occasion than it demands or than you can endure without embarrassment. How I have wished sometimes that I belonged to some other race, lived in another age, when breadth and depth of feeling were no embarrassment and to express them was a common joy! I am not a fool—at school, at college, and afterward in business, I proved that—yet too often I have behaved like a fool. Because my wits would be drowned in my emotions. Time after time I have condemned people for not feeling enough when I knew only too well that I felt too much, that I secretly envied them—you, Nina, for the light but sure hand you had upon the rein while I was plunging and bolting—you, Stuart, for the clear air, the bracing height, of your intellect—you, Matthew—but no, I never envied you, my dear, because I shared your triumphs. And because I hadn't the wits—or never used the wits God gave me—of course I had to lose you, as a woman if not as a friend. *Of course—of course*—notice how often I have to cry *Of course*—always so pitifully wise after the event. Feeling is not enough. Oh—how I would like to set that up in letters of fire where every blobbering girl could see their blaze! To feel is not to live, but only to be at the mercy of life, which, like so many of its people, merely despises those who rush blindly at it, lost in their emotion. What use is it that the engine races if there is no hand upon the wheel, no eye above it? I have had to talk to girls—too many of them—discussing their prospects, giving them good advice—and never once have I had the sense and honesty to tell them not to try and live through their emotions, to tell them to beware of feeling that is not guided by thought, that dulls their intuition, that robs them even of the pure joy of sensation. Never once did I tell them that the world is filled with traps for woman's emotion, or how artfully she's encouraged to

82

blind herself, and that even love itself—this love, love, love, that makes the world go round and annually declares a billion dollar dividend—is best not left to shaded lights, soft violins, fading close-ups of kisses—will not taste good unless it knows some cool self-discipline.

NINA

Sometimes I think the greatest fault of the women of our race is that too many of them never understand that. They know that falling in love belongs to Romance, but do not realize that enduring love must have the discipline of classic art. So they go straight from illusion to disillusion. All that is true. But surely you wrong yourself, dear Harriet, when you try to make us see you as a tear-stricken sentimental blunderer. We all know such women—and run from them —but you're not one of them.

HARRIET

For once, Nina, I must tell you you're too kind. This is the Moment of Truth—

STUART (*cutting in*)

Ah—that admirable image of the bullfighters! So now—that wounded bull, the Ego, sinks to the reddened sand, and self-knowledge, coming from God knows where, prepares to lean upon its thin bright blade.

HARRIET

Yes, this is the Moment of Truth—and it's too late for kindness.

MATTHEW

I don't believe it's ever too late for kindness. And that includes kindness to oneself. Harriet, I protest against your sudden cruelty to yourself. Remember what you once said to me—oh years ago—"Matthew, you're nicer than you think you are."

HARRIET

Yes, I remember, Matthew. It was probably the wisest thing I ever said to you. But if you feel, as you all seem to do, that now I'm giving a false picture of myself, ill-drawn and ugly through the sheer force of self-contempt, that only helps to prove my point, for this very caricature comes out of an excess of feeling. I've been remembering my very last day at college. It was winter; there had been snow but it had turned to dark slush; there was no color anywhere; the college looked like the last impression from some worn engraving; the whole February afternoon might have been imprisoned in some dark and dripping tunnel. As I went along for my final interview with our old principal, I felt infinitely forlorn. I had to wait awhile, where the cold drops fell from the eaves, to try to calm myself, before entering the lighted hallway to her room. She gave me tea and spoke about my plans. Then when it was time for me to go—and I was wondering if I would have to rush blindly from the room— she said, "Harriet, I know how you feel about leaving us, and I share some of your regret. But I have very few hours left, and you have wasted one of them. We women must command our emotions or we shall be enslaved by them. Look—here is something intended specially for you." And she gave me an open salt cellar made of iron, like the iron ornaments that German women wore after they had given their gold and silver for the War of Liberation against Napoleon. "Yes, Harriet," she said, as I tried to thank her for it. "Salt and iron. We shan't meet again, so keep this to remind you of what I said about our emotions. For our minds need salt and iron." And now I know how right, how wise, she was, that fragile, indomitable old woman. And because I have allowed myself to float on tides of feeling, I have even robbed myself of the husband, the children, the close friends, to whom I might have given myself emotionally, for too much unguided feeling creates its own blundering embarrassments, its sharp repulsions. Until in the end I had to spread a huge false pity over continents I'd never seen, on whole races that meant nothing to me deep at heart. I was Harriet—oh so conscientious a citizen of the world—so widely sensitive—so noble—forever vaguely doing good. Without salt. Without iron. Wasting—wasting—wasting the hours.

NINA

Matthew, say something to her.

MATTHEW

To her—yes—and to you and Stuart too. If, as I believe—and now hope, having brought you here—that that boat comes for me, little worth saving will be lost. What you said earlier, each of you, was true, and cut deeper than you thought. This doesn't mean that my reply was false, that I never believed my own defense. For I still believe—and would mutter it with my dying breath—that Man must be the changer, the maker, the creator, that we are here to master the earth. But Man means all men, using such gifts and skills as they possess, and above all those men—who seem to be dying out of the world rather than being born into it— who have some balance between muscle and brain and heart, who wish to widen and enlarge our human life because they themselves have enjoyed and love it. But not men like me. Remember what I say. This is my testament. Not men like me—for we are dangerous. We are the evil wizards, the warlocks, of this age. Using some dark intuitive power, we make our lucky guesses, and then drive ourselves and everybody else, with a maniac's undivided will and energy, to realize, in steel and stone and the pattern of men's lives, these glimpses of a future that perhaps nobody wants. For we do not know what we want. How can I know what I want of life? Tell me—how can I?

STUART

No, Matthew, now you're going too fast for us. Didn't I say, a little while ago, that because you know where you're going and what you want, in a world of doubt and indecision, you can almost hypnotize the rest of us into obedience?

MATTHEW

Oh yes, yes, yes—I know the company plan, the agreed objective, the immediate target—to use the jargon of the boardrooms. I know, better than most, that when I am at point A on the map I must proceed within a given time to point B. I know those things so well because I know so little else. But what I want of life—what other men should have—the shape and

86

color of tomorrow's world—the inner quality of our
experience—I know less about these things than the
schoolboy Harriet says I am. Remember what you said,
much earlier, Stuart—that in your view mine wasn't
a life but something like a one-man idiotic relay race,
and that I was the richest man you knew—also the
poorest. Poorest in what? I can answer for you—poorest in the quality of my experience, in my response
to that real world which Nina loves. I drive so hard
along the road because there's so little on either side I
want to see. You asked me what I was racing for, but
it may be that I'm not running *toward* anything but
away from something, that a host of men and women
are tumbling on behind a leader who isn't hurrying
them toward the Promised Land but is merely making
his escape in a blind panic. Nina has said that I shovel
the hours, the days, into the furnace of my impatience
and dissatisfaction; and if that is true—if I treat Time
as the enemy when it alone gives us the real world to
explore and to enjoy, the bare boughs of winter, the
summer grass—then I can ask again, How should I
know what I want of life? How can I shape, out of my
failure, my despair of flesh-and-blood living, the lives
of other men? Yet that is what we do, we sorcerers
who are so dangerous. For consider the world we're
making, and notice how we succeed—oh not con-
sciously, which would be safer, but by way of some
dark hidden plan—in robbing other men of what we
lack ourselves, in taking the tang and bloom out of
their experience, in blunting the edge of individuality,
in substituting some gray fodder for the hard sweet
nut of life that men used to crack between their teeth.
And when you stare at one of our giant new creations,

87

all steel and concrete and electric eyes, with every human twist and stain ironed out, you have taken a peep into our minds. But only into some fluorescent-lighted upper level, for far below, where the old darkness remains, a pitiful creature gropes and cries, "Lost—lost—lost!" and weeps with fear or rage. I tell you there are those of us, whose eyes across their desks have made me shrink and wonder, who out of their snarling disappointment, their fury with this life, would turn your towns into huge termitaries, and leave the world they hate an iron anthill.

HARRIET

But you are not one of them, Matthew. You have just told us so.

MATTHEW

No, your earlier guess at me was near the truth. I am not a man, a whole man, with an intellect warmed by feeling, with emotion guided by thought, with every intuition lodged in the real world that sensation gives us. Where are such men?

STUART

Secure forever in the timeless building that locked me out—the truly great, the noble sons of Heaven and Earth, for whom the mob exists—simply to serve and praise. But what are you then?

MATTHEW

I am in my essence only a boy, and even younger than the one that Harriet guessed at. A very small bewildered boy, who was told, by a mischievous farm lad, that three miles down the road, where the two

old elms cast their shadows on what was left of the
common, a kindly magician was giving away pony
carts to any boy who asked for one. So off I went, on a
desperate long hot trudge, to find no magician, no
pony carts, only a daft old woman who cackled malev-
olently when she saw my tears. And I swear to you
I've been searching ever since for that magic pony
cart, and in the world that wouldn't let me have it I've
plundered continents. So now you see who's been
driving you on—not a mature man but an angry child.
Not in the fantasies, the Aladdin's palaces of power,
but in the real world where men might begin to grow
old like wine, I have failed. So let the boy go: already
he has lived too long.

NINA (*after pause*)

How savagely you have attacked yourselves, Matthew, Harriet and Stuart. You make me think of those
Christian flagellants who ran through the cities of
Europe lashing their own backs with knotted scourges.
In spite of my closeness to you, my husband and
dearest friends, I am not going to lacerate myself—
because having made smaller claims I have less to
retract. I claimed only to have been happy, to have
enjoyed my life. That is true. I enjoyed the childhood
in which I am still rooted, my silly girlhood, and I
have relished—oh how I have relished—my life as a
woman. I would not shed a single January to Decem-
ber of them all. They have brought me much pain, it is
true. I have known the guilty vacancy of ceasing to
love, and the mortification and bitterness of ceasing
to be loved. I have known the anguish, I believe the
greatest possible to woman, of death intervening at

love's height. But don't think me abominable if I say that I have fed on all these cruel things as well as on happiness. I have grown fat on experience. My senses have gone out and in like bees bringing home nectar. I have joined myself with the whole world, sharing its darkness as well as its light, its trivialities equally with its splendors. Matthew said there must be conflict: I would go so far as to glory in the clash of opposites. There must be emotion and coolness; there must be mountain dawns and maggots squirming in filth. These conflicts are beyond the reach of human morality: they are as natural a part of life as death itself. That is why I accept them, glory in them, and am ready to enrich myself with whatever falls to my lot. And not for myself alone. We gather in innocent selfishness, we who live by the senses, but then we offer our booty to those who need it. You three need it—to nourish your intellect, your vaulting imagination, the nobility of your heart. It has taken five hundred million years, you said, to raise these human flowers from primeval ooze. Yes, and through all those cloudy aeons it has been the senses that have drawn them upward. When jawless fishes, fantastically finned and bearded, swarmed in the ancient oceans, the light and the looming shadows, the hazy intimations of forms and textures, that their eyes and slender feelers recorded were already preparing the stuff of a poet's images. When reptiles crawled from the water and felt mud and stones beneath their claws and sunshine on their scales, they too helped in this raising of the human mind. Then your own humble ancestors, the creatures of the trees—their long narrow hands that registered the roundness, the solidity of branch and nut—they were making possible your cleverness, Stuart. Their leathery embraces, the suckling and carrying of their young, these sensations underlie your deepest feelings, Harriet. The quick ear, nose and eye that warned of danger and led to the leadership of the horde, there is the source of your power and intuitions, Matthew. Yes, we gatherers of sensation, we still represent the elemental stuff from which mankind has built its house and lighted its lamps. We are your link with the sea and earth from which your proud qualities have grown; without us they would parch and wither.

STUART

Yes, Nina, yes! Didn't I say myself that the brain would wither? It is true, we need you.

NINA

And yet I find myself strangely willing to die. I am ready, even eager, to be your Iphigenia, to be the sacrifice that will allow the rest of you to set sail from Dragon's Mouth. Perhaps it is because I have so much desire for shapeliness, for perfection of form, that I want to cut short my life before it blurs—to die while I am still in possession of the rose, while heads still turn in the street. Perhaps too it is because we elementary human beings die more easily, more nearly like animals. Living from day to day we lack the purpose, the length of vision, to recognize the whole trajectory of life. We have no will to fight for things or against them along its whole course, from rise to fall.

MATTHEW

But, my darling, you are Nina, not just one of a kind.

91

STUART

I wonder. Didn't we begin by doubting our individuality?

MATTHEW

Not I. Yet I have learnt one thing from our boasting and our self-reproaches. We four, so profoundly different, are held together by our unlikeness.

HARRIET (*moves down between* NINA *and* STUART)

I think we stand at the four points of the compass.

NINA

We complement and so complete one another.

HARRIET

Like North, South, East and West, we embrace the globe, the globe of human personality.

NINA

And if there is any larger mind, comprehending and moving the world, it should appreciate us, and perhaps even now is feeding on our experience.

STUART (*harshly*)

But is about to remove one of us, one of the four quarters so necessary to each other.

HARRIET

Stuart, you are still too dry, too harsh. Allow yourself some tenderness. . . .

MATTHEW

Out of tonight you may yet write your masterpiece. . . .

NINA

Open yourself to the night . . . look at the stars, the moon sinking, and the fishermen sailing home. . . .

STUART (*goes closer to Harriet.
All four are now using the two center mikes*)

Very well, I accept. I will rein in my thoughts. But you must do the same, each one of you. Each must curb his own excess.

HARRIET

I will show you where to find warmth if you will show me where in myself to dig for salt and iron.

MATTHEW

Each of us can discover the other three in ourselves. It is a trust.

NINA

But after tonight there will not be four.

MATTHEW

That is why it is a trust, and a sacred one. So the three who are left must seek to enrich their being, to extend their experience, so that what was most real in the one who dies will live. Can we do it?

NINA

I think we can.

HARRIET

I think we have made a pact—even though we are being very metaphysical. . . .

STUART

What better time for men to be metaphysical than

93

when Death sends for them. (*Pointing left.*) Listen—
you can hear his messenger—

> (*They all look. The motorboat is heard, rapidly approaching.*)

MATTHEW

Yes, there it is. Shall we meet it together?

> (*The boat noise comes up to a roar as they look gravely toward it; the lights are faded almost out and a bright little spot comes up from the left, brightening and fading with the noise of the motorboat. When it stops there is a moment's blackout and silence.*)

EPILOGUE

WHILE suggesting that this platform play of *Dragon's Mouth* makes a step toward a promising new dramatic form, we have not failed to see it also as one current within a much broader movement. This is a trend back toward an enjoyment of words, whether they are listened to for the sake of their sound and imagery, or for the totally different pleasure of debate—the tossing to and fro of ideas. Can it be that we humans have an urge to exercise all our faculties and will react if some are starved and others glutted? Ours is a generation which has had visual images poured upon it from cinema, television and the illustrated press; which the instruments of mass communication have flooded with language used either lifelessly or with actual degradation. As for the contemporary theater itself, dramatists have sternly disciplined themselves to find expression through the everyday idiom of modern speech. Yet here is this reviving love of words, shown in a host of ways from the popularity of Brain Trusts and Dickens readings to the explosion of enthusiasm for Christopher Fry.

The appeal of Fry is perhaps the most significant of all, for it depends upon the lure of words for their own sake. Probably good debate has always had a ready audience, but here the public shows itself eager for an elaborately iced verbal confection designed to please ear and imagination.

There is no doubt about the general trend, but within it we have claimed something new for *Dragon's Mouth* and must support our claim by considering what distinguishes it as a form, what are its peculiar advantages and limitations. Some critics have accepted it as a new form but found it to be a lamentable one; some have accepted it as a new form and seen in it great promise for the future; others have accepted it as good entertainment but have denied it any novelty. With such striking lack of agreement among the critics there must be room for further comment.

Here, then, is a form in which the players remain in more or less fixed positions and speak a great part of their lines not to one another within the closed world of the stage but out to the audience. It is these two things which constitute the significant peculiarities of the form. The absence of scenery and of costume naturally made much of by the popular press is of great economic interest and of value in enabling performances to be played away from theaters, but dramatically means very little.

Foremost among the limitations imposed by this convention must be that it forbids both free action on the stage and similarly the development of a strong narrative plot. If there is to be a narrative it has to be presented, we believe, as a recollection of past events mounted as a vignette within the dramatic movement of the piece. Linked with this is the problem of keeping to the unities of time and place. It is rash to dogmatize as yet, but it would appear that the form demands they should be kept. It might be acceptable for centuries or continents to separate the acts; it would surely not be acceptable to the imagination if players left their appointed places on the boards and returned after a few minutes to what the program insisted was, let us say, "The conservatory in the same house, ten days later."

How far the form sets a limit to characterization is a more subtle and interesting problem. Evidently some of the most usual means of developing character on the stage must be forfeited together with action and narrative. The tragic fall of the hero through his own fault can hardly be compassed any more than the out-wittings and humiliations of a comic plot. On the other hand by change of pressure in the situation, such as we contrived in *Dragon's Mouth*, it is easy enough to make the characters reveal different sides of their nature: that is to say while it would seem impossible to develop a character in a linear way by making him walk along the length of a plot, he can be made to expose hidden facet after facet by being twisted round where he stands. How far can the characters thus exposed be brought into active relationship with one another? By references to the past, by tensions either concealed or openly avowed, existing relationships can be quite powerfully expressed, but we believe that any direct, active relationship between the characters on the stage, any violent emotional interchanges would be very ill-suited both to the static presentation and to the outward contact of players with audience.

At this point, however, the problem of character-ization leads us directly from the limitations to the advantages of the present convention. The very re-striction of the linear development of character

97

through action and active personal relationships allows a much fuller development of another kind—an expression of the nature of men and women, of the quality of their being and their experience immediately through words. If the dramatist is capable of it, this form allows a return to the verbal tradition of the Elizabethans in which it may be said a character *is* his "voice." How much of our comprehension of many of the creations of the Elizabethan stage come not from their actions, emotions or ideas and the talk which accompany them, but from the flow of their speech, from the words and images they employ.

This characterization by "voice" can only be achieved where action does not always rush the characters along or the need for realism clip their language. It demands a temporal spaciousness in which speeches can flower complete in themselves and sometimes spring from a level deep enough to allow the unconscious to affect words and images. To my mind these speeches whether they are concerned with events recollected, with descriptions, emotional analysis or unabashed oratory are the most important advantage offered by the present form both for characterization in the special sense described and for their own sake, as set pieces within the play and challenging actors to a subtle exercise of their art.

I have included oratorical speeches in this category, but in so far as they are concerned with intellectual ideas and arguments they relate also to the other leading advantage of the "platform play"—the opportunity it gives for debate. It is debate with the special advantages that, while its intelligence and wit are limited only by the capacity of the dramatist, it goes out to the listeners in such a way as to make them half believe in its spontaneity. Certainly in *Dragon's Mouth* we have found many not unsophisticated members of the audience who failed to distinguish between an actor's performance and the point of view he was expressing, so fully did they identify themselves with one or another of the characters on the stage.

Finally one asks, would the platform play be suited to poetic drama? Surely it would, were there poetic dramatists equipped to write for it! But whereas the fantastic settings and stories of Christopher Fry's plays allow him to get away with a very considerable amount of merely decorative verse, it seems that this form would demand poetry of a quality few indeed could command. On the other hand the size and freedom of the set speeches should make them a good vehicle for poetic feeling.

It is time to turn from the general to the particular. How far did Mr. Priestley and I succeed in adapting ourselves to the limits of our chosen form and in exploiting its advantages? Although Charles Laughton's production of *Don Juan in Hell* had suggested our enterprise, we did not, as some critics have assumed, imagine that we could achieve Shavian brilliance of wit and dialogue. We knew we must try instead to have more feeling in our piece and also to make a richer use of words, a more definite return to the verbal tradition.

Clearly, then, we had need of a strong situation, and one threatening enough to release tongues and emotions. In order, as I have suggested, to be able to twist round the static character and reveal unexpected facets we also wanted a change in our situation. The simple device we adopted of a cruising party first vaguely threatened by a deadly disease and then certainly condemned to face it satisfied these requirements while remaining sufficiently undistinguished and unrealistic not to demand too much attention. Words were the thing and we did not want our situation developing into an assertive plot. At the same time, however, it would be a dangerous mistake to suppose that a platform play could be successful if it were merely a conversation piece. Had the use of language in *Dragon's Mouth* been very much better than it is, it still would not have held an audience for two hours without Mr. Priestley's practiced dramatic craftsmanship.

Partly to give more shape, partly because verbal characterization was one of our aims, we determined to impose a psychological pattern upon that of the situation. Here again we did not want the pattern to be assertive, but we made our four characters represent the four "functions" of Jung—that is to say Thinking, Feeling, Sensation and Intuition.

As so few critics have detected this Jungian element, it is worth saying a few words about it here. Jung's belief is that all human beings have elements of all these functions contained in them, but always with one or two dominant and the others less developed. If one function is so absolutely dominant in the personality that the others are held altogether in abeyance then an incomplete human being will result. Jung therefore sees it as the moral duty of all in that condition to strengthen their undeveloped functions and so achieve the "fully integrated personality."

Needless to say, we did not wish to insist on this

psychological theory and during the first part of *Dragon's Mouth* kept it very much in the background. In the second half, however, when under duress the four begin to criticize themselves they expose their weakness—the excessive, unbalanced development of their dominant functions. If one wishes to push the interpretation so far, one could say this weakness explains why Stuart's intellect has made him no more than a rather arid scholar, why Matthew, the powerful intuitive, is a businessman and not a great artist and why Harriet has frustrated the very quality of feeling that she has in excess. The monotony of the four-square pattern in which all the characters having boasted in the first part turn to revile themselves in the second is relieved by Nina, the sensationist. She holds to her unambitious claim abundantly to have enjoyed her life through the exercise of her senses. The theoretical justification for this dramatically useful exception is that while the higher faculties cannot possibly flourish unless nourished by the senses, sensation, the most primitive faculty, can do very well without its senior partners.

The same Jungian concept of the four functions also provides a basis for the closing scene; the four characters know that one of them is to die, and their mutual promise to "rediscover" him or her in themselves can be taken as an affirmation of the need to integrate the personality—even while at the same time it represents a simple declaration of close friendship, which is the sense in which most people have accepted it.

Throughout we tried to keep the psychological fabric sufficiently transparent for the characters to

show as more than mere types, though plainly we sacrificed something of character in the round. As com-
pensation the use of the four types added to the variety
of what I have called verbal characterization. Thus
Stuart could reveal himself in precise and detailed
descriptive speeches; Nina through scenes and other
sensuous experiences vividly recalled; Harriet in emotionally charged memories of her youth; Matthew in
oratorical expression of his intuitive understanding of
life. I think it can be said that if they are not fully
realized in the round, and they are not, these characters
show a highly individual and often interesting surface texture and coloring, and that we have gone some
way to making them reveal the quality of their being
through their "voices."

As for the relationships between the four, from the
outset we accepted the limitations that forbade emotional exchanges of any intensity between the characters on the stage. We were content to show Matthew
and Nina as well and truly married and for the rest to
rely on recollections of past emotional passages to
provide an understanding of the currents running
between them. In this way we showed Stuart's per-
sistent and fruitless interest in Nina; Harriet's old
and now slightly embittered love for Matthew; and
Matthew's power over them all. Enough to hold them
together and to prepare for the close where they
recognize that they have always been bound by their
unlikeness, that is to say by their need to find in one
another what was atrophied in themselves.

I hope that reading the text makes it clear that this
idea of the need for one another of the four functions
is not, as several critics assumed, the same as the con-

vergence of personality expressed in Mr. Priestley's *Music at Night*. They remain essentially opposite types, but pledged to rescue their submerged functions in order to strengthen their several qualities of being.

For the rest, one of the most important problems both in writing and producing was to secure a harmonious and if possible even exciting movement between the talk and repartee exchanged between the characters and the speeches and appeals directed to the audience. Once or twice we made one character speak to the audience referring to the other three as instances of what he is saying. This is a means for drawing the audience into the dramatist's confidence which might be cunningly extended. There is no doubt that the whole theater did respond both to the set speeches addressed to them and to the debates in which they were being invited to take sides. In some towns in the provinces the battle between the sexes roused cheers and counter-cheers in the auditorium. Everywhere members of the audience said that their very enjoyment, the close attention demanded, left them exhausted by participation.

Dragon's Mouth is an early effort to achieve a form of writing for the stage—any stage, not only those found in theaters—which we hope will have many more perfectly realized successors. We could have been far wittier and carried more intellectual weight; we could have possessed higher poetic quality and achieved a much neater dramatic construction. Yet we have been extraordinarily well received both by our audiences and critics. With few exceptions, we have been praised by those whose praise we value and abused by those whose abuse we can wear among our laurels.

The actors continue to declare they find *Dragon's Mouth* most interesting and satisfying to perform; we as authors have had every kind of experience from it—trying and exhilarating, serious and funny, but none willingly to be forgone. We hope that our readers, whether or not they have seen a stage performance, will have got some satisfaction from following the text.

JACQUETTA HAWKES